Kenneth E. Boccafola, THE REQUIREMENT OF PERPETUITY
FOR THE IMPEDIMENT OF IMPOTENCE

T0126815

# Analecta Gregoriana

Cura Pontificiae Universitatis Gregorianae edita
Vol. 200. Series Facultatis Iuris Canonici: Sectio B, n. 35

KENNETH E. BOCCAFOLA

# THE REQUIREMENT OF PERPETUITY FOR THE IMPEDIMENT OF IMPOTENCE

UNIVERSITÀ GREGORIANA EDITRICE

ROMA 1975

KENNETH E. BOCCAFOLA

# THE REQUIREMENT OF PERPETUITY
# FOR THE IMPEDIMENT OF IMPOTENCE

Università Gregoriana Editrice
ROMA 1975

IMPRIMI POTEST

Romae, die 13 octobris 1975

R. P. HERVÉ CARRIER, S. I.
*Rector Universitatis*

Con approvazione del Vicariato di Roma in data 20 Ottobre 1975

TYPIS PONTIFICIAE UNIVERSITATIS GREGORIANAE — ROMAE

# INTRODUCTION

The problem of the "curability" of impotence is a perennial one for ecclesiastical judges. It would seem that such a problem, medical in nature, would decrease in inverse ratio to the progress made by medical science over the years. By relying on the more precise testimony of their medical experts, judges of ecclesiastical courts, one would think, should be able to come to much more exact conclusions about the perpetual or temporary nature of the particular impotent condition in question.

Rather, quite the contrary has occurred. The problem of "curability" is even more acute than previously, for modern jurisprudence has seen its connection with questions beyond the boundaries of the impediment of physical impotence. Canon 1068, No. 1, of the Code of Canon Law determines the characteristics which the physical condition of impotence must have to be the diriment impediment of impotence:

> Impotentia *antecedens* et *perpetua*, sive ex parte viri sive ex parte mulieris, sive alteri cognita sive non, sive absoluta sive relativa, matrimonium ipso naturae iure dirimit.

These same conditions have been seen by some recent writers as applicable to a new *caput nullitatis* which has a close relationship to the diriment impediment of impotence.[1] Recent

---

[1] J. R. KEATING, referring to Huizing's definition of the impediment of moral impotence: "He calls it impotence because its invalidating force on the marriage contract is identical with the invalidating force of the traditional impediment of impotence in C. 1608...," in "Sociopathic Personality," *The Jurist*, 25 (1965), 435. Cf. also JOHN T. FINNEGAN, "The Current Jurisprudence Concerning the Psychopathic Personality," *The Jurist*, 27 (1967), 443: "We have called it the impediment of moral impotence, for the concept of the inability to assume rights and obligations of the marriage contract is nothing more than the impediment of impotence extended to all the essential *iura-debita* of the contract." Cfr. also *ibid.*, p. 450; JOSÉ PINTO, "De matrimonii nullitate ob psychicam incapacitatem fidem coniugalem servandi," *Periodica*, 61 (1972), 440:

scholarship and the development of jurisprudence have brought
to the fore a new source of nullity for which the authors themselves have not yet found a consistent terminology: "moral
impotence," "psychic incapacity," "psychic irregularity," "consti-
tutional incapacity," "incapacitas assumendi onera," are some
of the terms used.[2] The question, therefore, arises whether the
requirements of C. 1068 for physical impotence must also be
applied to this new, related source of nullity. "Curability," or
more exactly the meaning of the requirement of perpetuity, is
a real problem being discussed by Church Tribunal personnel.[3]

    The object of this dissertation, then, will be to study in
detail the requirement of the perpetuity of impotence contained
in C. 1068, No. 1. The first chapter will consist of an historical
inquiry into the origin and the reason for this requirement of
perpetuity. Chapter Two will seek to properly understand the
meaning of perpetuity as it has been presented historically.
Such an attempt at a deeper understanding of the meaning of
perpetuity will necessarily involve a synthesis of the elements
found in three historical periods. The result, a descriptive
definition of perpetuity, will be presented in Chapter Three,
and compared with a related notion from the field of moral
theology. The specific contribution of the modern period, par-
ticularly of modern Rotal jurisprudence, will be dealt with in
the fourth and last Chapter.

    This work will thus constitute a monograph illustrating the
origin, meaning and function of the requirement of perpetuity

---

"Cum vero impedimentum hoc e iure naturae dimanet, eodem modo
ac impotentia coeundi viget, scilicet incapacitas debet esse antecedens
ac perpetua."

    [2] Cf. PETRUS HUIZING, "Some Proposals for the Formation of Matri-
monial Law: Impediments, Consent, Form, I," *The Heythrop Journal*,
7 (1966), 161-182; JOHN R. KEATING, *The Bearing of Mental Impairment on
the Validity of Marriage* (Rome, 1963), p. 187; J. T. FINNEGAN, "The Capacity to Marry," *The Jurist*, 29 (1969), 141; LAWRENCE WRENN, *Annulments*
(Hartford, [2]1972), Preface to the second edition; MARION J. REINHARDT,
GERARD J. ARELLA, "Essential Incompatibility as Grounds for Nullity of
Marriage," *The Catholic Lawyer*, 16 (1971), 173-187; URBANO NAVARRETE,
" 'Incapacitas assumendi onera' uti caput autonomum nullitatis matri-
monii," *Periodica*, 61 (1972), 47-80.

    [3] M. J. REINHARDT, "The Incidence of Mental Disorder," *Studia Cano-
nica*, 6 (1972), 209-225; EUGENE J. FITZSIMMONS, in the Animadversions of
the Defender of the Bond in the case of Vogle vs. Wylie, Tribunal of the
Diocese of Camden, N.J. Prot. No. M-69/43; CHARLES DILLEN, Defender of
the Bond of the Tribunal of the Archdiocese of Detroit, Michigan, in
private correspondence with M. J. REINHARDT, February 21, 1973.

for the impediment of impotence. It is hoped that this study will be of some assistance to ecclesiastical judges and Tribunal members who must concern themselves with the provisions of C. 1068. Even more importantly, however, it is hoped that this work will contribute to the progress of canonical studies by providing a point of departure for further investigation into the question whether the requirement of perpetuity must be applied to cases, such as those of psychic incapacity, which are outside the strict limits of the impediment of impotence.

An expression of sincere gratitude is due to the Most Rev. Walter P. Kellenberg, D.D., Bishop of Rockville Centre, who enabled me to pursue my canonical studies at the Pontifical Gregorian University and to publish this dissertation; to the Rev. Urbano Navarrete, Professor of Canon Law at the Gregorian University and moderator of this dissertation, who directed me by his many helpful suggestions and with constant patient understanding; to Most Rev. Boleslao Filipiak, Dean of the Sacred Roman Rota, who graciously permitted me to consult the unpublished sentences of the Rota; and to the Rev. Egidio Turnaturi, who assisted me in my research.

I would also like to express my deep appreciation to Rev. Msgr. Marion J. Reinhardt, Chief Judge of the Tribunal of the Diocese of Brooklyn, for his suggestion of the topic of this dissertation and for his unfailing help and encouragement; to Rev. Eugene Fitzsimmons, Defender of the Bond of the Tribunal of the Diocese of Camden, N.J., and to Rev. Charles Dillen, Defender of the Bond of the Tribunal of the Archdiocese of Detroit, for their helpful advice.

Finally, I offer heartfelt gratitude to my fellow priests at the Casa Santa Maria — especially to Rev. Michael Sernett, Rev. Richard Viladesau, Rev. George Ryan, Rev. Ronald Bryda, Rev. Robert Sanson, Rev. John Ross and Rev. Edward Adams — whose help and understanding have been of such great value to me.

Rome, July 1, 1974

K. E. B.

# TABLE OF CONTENTS

# ABBREVIATIONS

| | | |
|---|---|---|
| *D.* | = | *Digesta* |
| *Dec.* | = | *Sacrae Romanae Rotae Decisiones seu Sententiae* |
| *DDC* | = | *Dictionnaire de droit canonique* |
| *DTC* | = | *Dictionnaire de théologie catholique* |
| *EIC* | = | *Ephemerides Iuris Canonici* |
| *IDE* | = | *Il diritto ecclesiastico* |
| *ME* | = | *Monitor ecclesiasticus* |
| *PL* | = | *Patrologia latina* |

NOTE: In the commentaries on the *Decretals*, the material on the impediment of impotence is found in the *rubrica* or *titulus*: *de frigidis et maleficiatis et impotentia coëundi*. For the sake of brevity, we have used the most common designation for that title: tit. 15, except in those cases in which the edition used clearly indicates the contrary.

CHAPTER ONE

# AN HISTORICAL SURVEY OF JURIDICAL PERPETUITY AS A REQUIREMENT FOR THE DIRIMENT IMPEDIMENT OF IMPOTENCE

## A. ORIGIN AND DEVELOPMENT OF THE REQUIREMENT OF PERPETUITY

Before we can address ourselves to our primary question: what is the meaning of that adjective, *perpetual*, required of impotence in C. 1068, No. 1, we must first clearly understand the substantive which it modifies, viz. *impotence*. The close connection between perpetuity-impotence throughout this dissertation makes it extremely important to understand the precise signification of each, and the relationship between them.

Impotence, though derived from the natural law,[1] is quite a complex notion. The term comprehends both a situation of fact and a concept of law, a natural condition and a juridical impediment.[2]

It hardly seems necessary to point out that the condition of impotence is quite different in the case of the male than in that of the female.[3] A complete study of this condition would involve a discussion of the respective anatomical and physiological aspects of male and female impotence, an indication of the causes of each and the respective possibilities of cure.[4]

---

[1] C. 1068, No. 1.

[2] Cf. ROTAL decision c. SABATTANI, 10 April 1959, published in *ME* 84 (1959), 620: "Perpetuitas impotentiae est conceptus iuris, non merus eventus facti: ..." Cf. also PAUL HARRINGTON, "The Impediment of Impotency and the Notion of Male Impotency," *The Jurist*, 19 (1959), 52; cf. also pp. 30 and 42.

[3] Yet RUDOLPH ALLERS, M.D., Ph.D., is quite explicit in distinguishing the respective juridical consequences of absolute and relative impotence for each sex in "Some Medico-Psychological Remarks on C. 1068, 1081, 1087," *The Jurist*, 4 (1944), 351-380.

[4] Cf. JOHN J. BRENKLE, *The Impediment of Male Impotence with Special Application to Paraplegia* (Washington, D.C., 1963), pp. 1-47.

One would necessarily have to distinguish the condition of impotence from that of sterility; *impotentia coëundi* from *impotentia generandi*.

The complexities would scarcely be less were one to deal merely with the *impediment* of impotence. The writer would have to define the notion of impediment and the distinction between prohibiting and diriment impediments. Furthermore, he could not avoid a long treatise on the opinions of the authors as to what constitutes the canonical notion of the impediment of impotence; he would have to present the early opinions, the contribution made by the bull *Cum frequenter* of Pope Sixtus V, the effect of the influence of Gasparri, and the so-called modern opinion.[5]  Only then could he come to discuss the conditions necessary for the verification of the impediment in a particular case: antecedence and perpetuity.

But it is precisely this last point that is our object of study; we are seeking to discover the origin of this requirement of perpetuity, and its meaning as understood by the classic authors and in modern Rotal jurisprudence.  A complete treatment of the notion of impotence, itself, would, therefore, be beyond our scope here.

A general commonly agreed upon definition corresponding to the earlier almost popular understanding of the term will be quite sufficient for our purposes.[6]  In the words of St. Raymond of Pennafort, "Impotentia coeundi est vitium animi, vel corporis, vel utriusque, quo quis impeditur alii carnaliter commisceri."[7]

In short, impotence is the inability to have sexual intercourse; it consists in the lack of one or more of the following elements: erection of the penis, penetration into the vagina, and ejaculation therein.  Such a definition is descriptive of the condition, and at the same time at least satisfies the narrowest

---

[5] HARRINGTON, "The Impediment of Impotency," pp. 335-351; BRENKLE, *The Impediment of Male Impotence*, pp. 48-134.

[6] Gratian and his "auctoritates" use the following terms: "...numquam permixtione carnis conjuncti una caro effecti fuissent" C. 27, q. 2, c. 28; "...nubere non possunt" *ibid.*, c. 29; "...non possit coire" *ibid.*; "...impossibilitas coeundi" *ibid.*; "...non posse operam carni dantes commisceri" C. 33, q. 1, c. 2; "...non possunt naturaliter concordare" *ibid.*

[7] *Summa*, ed. H. Laget (Veronae, ²1744), lib. IV, tit. 16, p. 513.

interpretation of the impediment (i.e. that canonical impotence does not require *verum semen*).[8]

Finally it is important to realize that differences of opinion over the canonical definition of impotence will have no practical effect on the application of the requirement of perpetuity, for whatever definition of impotence one may hold, the requirement of perpetuity as described in this dissertation must be applied to it in order to fulfill the terms of C. 1068, No. 1.

## 1. *Presuppositions*

As we have seen, C. 1068, No. 1, establishes a requirement of perpetuity: "Impotentia antecedens et perpetua ... matrimonium ipso iure naturae dirimat." What do we mean by this "requirement of perpetuity"? Certainly, we cannot be speaking about "requiring" a natural condition; such a natural condition either would exist or would not; it could not be the object of any obligation. To speak of perpetuity as a requirement only makes sense in the context of the notion of impediment, i.e. something which either prohibits or prevents a marriage from coming into existence. In such a connection, the "requirement" of perpetuity means that the impediment of impotence will only exist and have its effect when one of the specific characteristics of the natural condition is this quality of perpetuity.

The existence of the requirement of perpetuity as an attribute of the diriment impediment of impotence, itself presupposes: 1) the existence of the impediment of impotence based on some law (natural or positive); 2) that such an impediment is a *diriment* impediment, i.e. one which nullifies rather than merely prohibits. Furthermore, before one can speak of a *diriment* or *nullifying* impediment, one must have a clear idea of the formation of the marriage bond, and of the moment that bond comes into existence.

---

[8] A general definition such as that given above is accepted as a starting point by Pietro Gasparri: "Praemittimus impotentiam quae irritat matrimonium esse impossibilitatem habendi copulam matrimonialem; idque omnes admittunt." *Tractatus canonicus de matrimonio*, I (Romae, [2]1932), n. 511. F. M. Cappello also agrees with such a preliminary definition: "Nomine *impotentiae* venit generatim incapacitas viri aut mulieris ad copulam *coniugalem* (quae *perfecta* communiter a D. D. vocari solet)." *Tractatus canonico-moralis de sacramentis*, V: *De matrimonio* (Romae, [7]1961), n. 342. Cf. E. REGATILLO, *Ius Sacramentarium* (Santander, [3]1960), n. 1257.

Consequently, the investigation of the origin of the requirement of perpetuity becomes quite a complex task. When we
find a reference to perpetuity we must immediately situate it
in the context of the theory of the formation of the marriage
bond and of the idea of impediment prevalent at that time.
Accordingly, it is necessary to summarize briefly the two general
theories on the formation of the marriage bond and explain
their relation to the idea of diriment impediment and to the
requirement of perpetuity.

### a) *The Requirement of Perpetuity in Relation to the "Copula" Theory*

The Church's teaching on marriage was the result of a long
process of evolution. The factors involved in this process were:
the teachings of Scripture, the writings of the Church Fathers
and also the cultural milieu of the times. Two traditions above
all played a part in the formation of the Latin Church's attitude
toward marriage: one was the tradition of Roman law which
emphasized "nuptias consensus, non concubitus, facit";[9] the
other was the influence of the scriptural phrase *"una caro"*,
reinforced by the tradition of the Germanic customary law
which recognized the act of sexual intercourse as an essential
element of marriage.[10]

Early medieval theological and canonical doctrine constantly
recognized the role of consent but hesitated to determine whether
this was the only necessary and sufficient element for the formation of a sacramental indissoluble matrimonial bond, or
whether the further element of *commixtio sexuum* must take
place to complete the process.

The "copula" theory was one solution adopted by Hincmar
(806-882), Archbishop of Rheims, and by Gratian and the canonical school of Bologna. In short, it taught that the marriage
bond was formed by a process involving successive moments:
that of the *coniugium initiatum* (arising from the consensual
aspects of the process — *desponsatio, coniugalis pactio, coniugalis fides*); that of the *coniugium ratum* brought about by the

---

[9] *D.* 35, 1, 15; *D.* 50, 17, 31.
[10] G. LE BRAS, "La doctrine du mariage chez les théologiens et les
canonistes depuis l'an mille," s.v. "Mariage," in *Dictionnaire de théologie catholique*, IX², col. 2137.

*copula carnalis* which perfects and stabilizes the juridical bond so that it is truly sacramental and indissoluble.[11]

The relationship of this theory to the problem of practical cases arising from the condition of impotence was relatively simple. Roman law had been familiar with cases of impotence and provided a solution by allowing divorce.[12] Such a solution granting perfect divorce, i.e. separation with the right to remarry, was quite in harmony with the copula theory. No conflict with the principle of indissolubility arose, because the divorce was not seen as breaking an already formed sacramental bond; rather it was merely a legitimate reason to halt the process of the formation of that bond which had been begun by the exchanging of consent.

The idea of a diriment impediment of impotence is inconsistent with the copula theory just described. An impediment may be either a prohibiting or a diriment impediment; the former forbids an act to take place, but does not affect the validity of the act, should it take place contrary to the law; the latter nulliifes the act, that is, it deprives of all juridic force any act performed contrary to the dictates of the law. Canonical axioms illustrate the difference: *prohibentia impediunt fieri, permittunt facta teneri; dirimentia vetant connubia facienda, facta retractent.*

Impotence, then, seen in the light of the copula theory was not an impediment nullifying a contract already entered into; rather, it was a *de facto* situation which happened to prevent the actual formation of the marriage. It was a natural condition physically preventing the act which formed the marriage bond, rather than an impediment of law preventing the transferral of rights and obligations which otherwise would have arisen from the valid act of consent. John Alesandro, speaking of Gratian's view of marital consummation, sums it up well:

> This attitude means that Gratian fails to distinguish between the nullity of a marriage because of antecedent and perpetual impotence and the dissolution of a valid, although *de facto*

---

[11] PIETRO A. D'AVACK, *Cause di nullità e di divorzio nel diritto matrimoniale canonico*, I (Firenze, ²1952), 26.

[12] G. OESTERLÉ, "Impuissance," *Dictionnaire de droit canonique*, V, col. 1262; M. CONTE A CORONATA, *Tractatus canonicus de Sacramentis*, III: *De matrimonio et de sacramentalibus* (Romae, ³1957), 372, n. 299; D'AVACK, *Cause*, p. 426.

unconsummated, marriage. *Impossibilitas coeundi* is merely
a ground, along with all the others, for dissolving a set of
mutual rights and obligations, which has not yet been trans-
formed into a *coniugium ratum*. Perpetual impotence means
that a marriage will never begin to exist because the completion of the essential matrimonial process by *copula carnalis*
is impossible. The significant element is *not* that the impotent person is incapable of contracting a valid matrimony
because of inability to fulfill the essence of marriage; the key
point is that such a person is not even capable of positing the
*de facto* element *necessary* to bring a marriage into existence
in the first place. [13]

We can therefore conclude that impotence, at this point, was
not yet a *diriment* impediment.[14]

Since the adherents of the copula theory did not look upon
impotence as a diriment impediment, they also were not yet
concerned with determining any characteristics necessary for
the verification of this impediment in a particular case.
Actually the requirement of perpetuity does not have much importance in the context of the copula theory. If the marriage
only comes into being at the moment of consummation, one
does not have to be concerned with the temporary or perpetual
nature of the impotence. Both temporary and perpetual are
at the moment of consummation *actual* impotence. It is this
actual impotence which *de facto* prevents the completion of the
marriage process and the consequent establishment of a valid,
indissoluble bond. Hence, there would be no reason for the
adherents of this theory to insist upon the perpetuity of impotence.

---

[13] JOHN ALESANDRO, *Gratian's Notion of Marital Consummation* (excerpts from a dissertation for the Pontificia Universitas Gregoriana)
(Rome, 1971), p. 84.

[14] Cf. A. DE SMET: "... nombre de docteurs, surtout parmi les parti-
sans de la *copulatheoria*, considérent l'impuissance, non comme un empêchement dirimant, mais plutôt comme une cause de dissolution *de
plano* du mariage non consommé." in *DTC*, VII², Col. 1438 s.v. "Impuissance." Also, A. ESMEIN - R. GENESTAL, *Le mariage en droit canonique*, I
(Paris, ²1929), 259; HARRINGTON, "The Impediment of Impotency," p. 30;
CONTE A CORONATA, *De matrimonio*, p. 373, n. 299; D'AVACK, *Cause*, p. 427,
n. 429. The opinion of F. Wernz - P. Vidal - P. Aguirre holding that impotence was considered a diriment impediment at this time in *Ius canonicum*, V: *Ius matrimoniale* (Romae, ³1946), 267, nota 24, is refuted by
Oesterlé, in "Impuissance," *DDC*, V, col. 1262.

b) *The Requirement of Perpetuity in Relation to the "Consent" Theory*

A quite different explanation of the formation of the marriage bond was provided by the theologians of the School of Paris. Their most famous spokesman, Peter Lombard, briefly recapitulated their theory by stressing the following points:

1. The efficient cause of marriage is the consent of the parties in the present.

2. Sexual intercourse (consummation) has no effect on the formation of the bond; it integrates and completes its symbolism.

3. After the consent of the parties presently expressed, the marriage is indissoluble.[15]

Such a doctrine wreaked havoc on the previous explanation given to divorce and had direct consequences on the solution of practical cases involving impotence, and on the very concepts of impotence and the perpetuity of impotence.

Divorce, understood as separation with the right to remarry, can be harmonized with the Church's teaching on the indissolubility of marriage only in two ways: either the divorce merely breaks up a marriage which had not yet attained the perfection of indissolubility, or the marriage was really *no* marriage because it was null and void *ab initio*. In other words, it had not been a true marriage involving indissolubility because some lack or defect had vitiated the true formation of the marriage bond; the bond only *appeared* to have been formed. This second alternative is actually the notion of diriment impediment. The distinction of diriment and prohibiting impediments was not a reflexive work of Canon Law but a gradual and hesitating development brought about by the solution of practical problems and an attempt to justify them according to a coherent doctrine.[16] Thus we can say that the change in attitude brought about by the consent theory gave great

---

[15] PETRUS LOMBARDUS, *Libri IV Sententiarum*, ed. cura PP. Collegii S. Bonaventurae ad Claras Aquas (Quaracchi, ²1916), II, lib. IV, d. 27, c. 3, p. 917: "Efficiens autem causa matrimonii est consensus, non quilibet, sed per verba expressus, nec de futuro, sed de praesenti.... Ex his apparet quod consensus, id est, pactio coniugalis, matrimonium facit; et *ex tunc* [emphasis mine] coniugium est, etiam si non praecessit vel secuta sit copula carnalis." For indissolubility, see *ibid.*, d. 26, c. 10, p. 924.

[16] ESMEIN-GENESTAL, *Le mariage en droit canonique*, p. 80.

impetus to the development of the idea of the diriment impediment of impotence.

Once the idea of diriment impediment had been established, canonists were soon led to point out the requirements and conditions under which this impediment would be verified. Hence, soon after the consent theory took hold, we find many more explicit references to the need for the perpetuity of impotence. The consequence of this change in attitude was, therefore, to make perpetuity an explicit requirement for the verification of the diriment impediment of impotence. The reasons why perpetuity came to be required will be discussed later, along with the various explanations of the nullifying force of impotence.

## 2. Historical Survey

### a) Theodore of Canterbury

The *Penitential of Theodore of Canterbury* (ca. 690), perhaps the earliest ecclesiastical document referring to the problem of impotence,[17] makes no mention of the *duration* of the man's impotent condition:

> Si vir et mulier coniunxerint se in matrimonio et postea dixerit mulier de viro non posse nubere cum ea, si quis poterit probare quod verum sit, accipiat alium.[18]

All that seems to be required is a need for proof of actually present impotence which would be a cause for perfect separation, i.e. with the right of the woman to remarry.

### b) Hincmar of Rheims

In a letter of Hincmar (806-882), Archbishop of Rheims, we have the first reference to the idea of permanence or perpetuity in connection with the separation of spouses due to impotence:

> Quod si per sortiarias, atque maleficias, occulto, sed numquam vel nusquam iniusto, Dominici iudicio permittente, et diabolo

---

[17] OESTERLÉ, "Impuissance," *DDC*, V, col. 1263; CONTE A CORONATA, *De matrimonio*, p. 372, n. 299; D'AVACK, *Cause*, p. 505.
[18] *Liber poenitentialis Theodori Cantuariensis*, lib. II, tit. 12, c. 33, in *Die Canones Theodori Cantuariensis und ihre Überlieferungsformen*, ed. Paul Finsterwalder (Weimar, 1929), p. 330.

operante, accidit, hortandi sunt quibus ista eveniunt, ut corde contrito, et spiritu humiliato, Deo et sacerdoti de omnibus peccatis suis puram confessionem faciant, et profusis lacrymis, ac largioribus eleemoysinis et orationibus, atque ieiuniis, Domino satisfaciant, ... et per exorcismos atque caetera medicinae ecclesiae munia, ministri Ecclesiae ... sanare procurent. Qui si forte sanare non potuerint, separari valebunt; sed post, quam alias nuptias expetierint, illis in carne viventibus, quibus iunctae fuerint, prioribus quos reliquerant, etiamsi possibilitas concumbendi eis reddita fuerit, reconciliari nequibunt. [19]

Here we have a case of impotence *ob maleficium*, impotence which does not seem to have any easily discernible natural cause and is therefore attributed to the action of the devil by means of a curse or spell. The belief in the efficacy of such spells was quite common in the Middle Ages; it was thought that the parties could remove this obstacle by suitable spiritual remedies.

The phrase "si forte sanare non potuerint, separari valebunt" seems to connote the idea of perpetuity since it could be interpreted as meaning: only a permanent or perpetual condition of impotence would justify the separation of the spouses.

However, when we situate this passage in the context in which it was found, and when we realize that Hincmar of Rheims was one of the strongest proponents of the copula theory, such an interpretation seems highly unlikely. Hincmar is simply stating here that the ecclesiastical authorities must use all prudent means in this case to determine whether there is actually a legitimate reason for the interruption of the marriage process which has been begun.[20] After all, in context, the whole difficulty might easily be cleared up by prayer, confession and true penance on the part of the spouses or by exorcisms on the part of the Church. On the other hand, the problem might be only a passing difficulty encountered because of extreme youth or the inexperience of the parties. In fact, it might all be due

---

[19] HINCMARUS REMENSIS, *Epistola ad Archiepiscopos Rodolfum et Frotarium, de nuptiis Stephani*, in *Patrologia latina*, ed. Migne, 126, col. 151; also contained in the *Decretum Gratiani*, C. 33, q. 1, c. 4.

[20] "Sed subtilis investigatio, et rationabilis discretio in his prius est adhibenda, utrum quasi naturalis in viris sit huiusmodi commistionis impossibilitas.... an hoc impedimentum operatione diaboli sicut fieri assolet, illis accidit." *PL*, 126, col. 151.

to a sense of guilt on the part of one of the spouses; such was the case of Count Stephen.[21]

A further argument that "si forte sanare non potuerint, separari valebunt" does not refer to the necessity of a condition of perpetual impotence is the fact that Hincmar explicitly states that the first marriage is not to be restored, *even if potency is actually shown to exist in the second marriage.* For if the words "si forte sanare non potuerint, separari valebunt" are to be understood as requiring the presence of a perpetual state of impotence, then the contrary position would also be true: ". . . si sanare potuerint, separari *non* valebunt." But this is expressly denied by the text: ". . . etiamsi possibilitas concumbendi eis reddita fuerit, reconciliari nequibunt." Therefore, the words do not seem to refer to a requirement of perpetuity, but simply to the fact that if consummation has not taken place, there are good grounds for separation. In this light and in accord with the copula theory, there would be no reason to demand the restoration of the first marriage if potency should actually happen to be regained at a later date.

### c) *Gratian*

The great teacher of the School of Bologna, dealing with the matter of impotence in his *Concordia discordantium canonum*, or *Decretum* as it is commonly known, also uses phrases that connote the idea of perpetuity. Causa 27, question 2, canon 28, uses phrases such as, "causa frigiditatis," "numquam", "vir frigidae naturae." C. 33, q. 1, c. 1, allows a wife to remarry but forbids an impotent husband to do so. It is because he is perpetually impotent? Likewise, C. 33, q. 1, c. 2, speaks of a man of "frigidae naturae" who could not "naturaliter concordare" with his wife. They are allowed to separate, but he must not remarry. If he does remarry, they must go back to each other and re-establish the first marriage. Why? One could answer: the impotence was merely temporary; only perpetual impotence nullifies; therefore, the first marriage was valid and must be restored. If Gratian and the author of the text reasoned in this manner,[22] it would seem to establish that perpetuity was seen

---

[21] *Ibid., passim.*

[22] Gratian says the author of C. 33, q. 1, c. 2, is Pope Gregory, writing to John, Bishop of Ravenna. Aemilius Friedberg in his edition of Gratian's *Decretum* in *Corpus Juris Canonici*, I (Lipsiae, ²1879) (photo

at that early date as an essential requirement of the nullifying force of impotence.

But from what we have said earlier about the concept of the formation of the marriage bond among the followers of the copula theory, such an interpretation is most unlikely.

What, then, is the correct interpretation of these references? Why does the marriage dissolved in C. 33, q. 1, c. 1, and that in c. 2 have to be restored if the impotent man is proved potent in a subsequent marriage?

Alesandro discusses the possible interpretations of the latter text and remarks that the "returned potency of the first husband provides the hindsight necessary to see that the justification of the dissolution (male impotence) never existed in the first place." [23]  This again seems to favor the requirement of perpetuity.  The Glossators, too, comment on the word *naturaliter*: "Naturaliter, id est, naturali frigiditate impediente.  Et est argumentum quod frigiditas est perpetuum impedimentum." [24]

However, I agree with what Alesandro has called a "more natural interpretation," [25] which would better accord with Gratian's theory of the formation of the marriage bond.  The marriage here must be restored, not *because* the impotence *was* only *temporary*, but *because the parties*, together with their *septima manu* witnesses *lied* to the Church authorities.  The presumption is, then, that the marriage had really been consummated and that the parties were guilty of perjury.  Indications supporting this are: 1) a truly impotent man would have no reason to attempt marriage again: "Nam si huic non potuit naturaliter concordare, quomodo alteri conveniet?";[26] 2) if he attempts to marry again it is evident that the only reason for the dissolution of the first marriage is his hatred of his first wife which leads him to perjure himself: "Igitur si vir aliam vult uxorem accipere, manifesta patet ratio, quia, suggerente diabolo odii fomitem, exosam eam habuit et idcirco eam dimittere mendacii falsitate molitur." [27]

---

offset edition, Graz, 1955), col. 1149, nota 14, indicates that the actual author is Rabanus Maurus in a letter to Heribald.

[23] ALESANDRO, *Gratian's Notion of Marital Consummation*, p. 67.

[24] *Glossa ordinaria* in C. 33, q. 1, c. 2 s.v. *naturaliter*.

[25] ALESANDRO, *Gratian's Notion of Marital Consummation*, p. 67.

[26] C. 33, q. 1, c. 2.

[27] *Ibid.*

A similar interpretation of the phrase "si forte sanare non potuerint, separari valebunt" in C. 33, q. 1, c. 4, is probable. As we have seen in the discussion of this text in its original by Hincmar of Rheims, the force of that phrase does not seem to have been concerned with the perpetuity of the impotence, but with the fact that dissolutions of even inchoate marriages must not be granted rashly. Perpetuity of impotence cannot be understod here as a requirement for the validity of the dissolution because it is explicitly stated that the second marriage should be maintained, even if potency should actually be regained. Furthermore, in the *dictum post* c. 4 of C. 33, q. 1, Gratian notes the contrary solutions given in c. 2 and in c. 4 of the same Causa. In the first case (c. 2) the first marriage of the parties must be restored. In the second situation (c. 4), the first marriage cannot be restored. Why? By juxtaposing these texts, Gratian insinuates that there are different juridical consequences arising from impotence due to a natural cause and impotence arising from a curse or spell. These different consequences were not based on the perpetuity or temporality of the impotence, but on the fact that a man under a spell could be quite rightly free of the crimes of perjury and hatred of his first wife even though he should be potent in a later marriage. On the other hand, one who said he was naturally impotent and then was found out not to be, must be considered a liar. Such a person could be considered as not having a sufficient reason to justify the dissolution of his marriage and thus not be deserving of the favor of an ecclesiastical dissolution of his *matrimonium initiatum*.

Before going on to view the writings of men who approached this problem from an entirely different outlook, it will be helpful here to briefly review the developments with regard to the impediment of impotence in this period before it was definitely established as a diriment impediment.

Even though this was the time of the predominance of the copula theory, still the various types of impotence were beginning to be distinguished and different juridical consequences taken into consideration. Cases of male impotence go back to the *Penitential of Theodore,* and if Friedberg is correct, the case of female impotence mentioned in C. 32, q. 7, c. 18, goes back as far as Rabanus Maurus (c. 775-865).

We note also the knowledge of the distinction between *natural* and that type of *accidental* impotence brought about by a spell, *maleficium*.   The logical consequence of this is the correlative distinction between *absolute* and *relative* impotence, which is implicitly recognized here by the permission to remain together in the second marriage granted in C. 33, q. 1, c. 4.

In this period and among the adherents of the copula theory, the question of *antecedent* and *subsequent* impotence is raised, not in connection with the act of consent, but with the act of carnal copulation which consummates the marriage. Any impotence that arises *after* the marriage has become absolutely indissoluble because consummated, has no effect on the marriage bond.   However, antecedent impotence, which prevents the completion of the marriage process, provides reason for dissolution, not so much because it is a diriment impediment, but because it *de facto*, whether temporary or permanent, prevents the *actual* formation of the marriage bond here and now by sexual intercourse.[28]

So, too, with the distinction between perpetual and temporary impotence.   We can justly say with Harrington that "the question of the temporary or permanent duration of the impotent condition was not a factor in the attitude of Gratian towards impotency." [29]   The concern of Hincmar and Gratian was not about the *duration* of the impotency, but about its *actual* presence which was reason enough for the reversal of the marriage process begun with the *desponsatio*.   They would therefore have no reason to seek a nullifying characteristic (perpetuity) to legitimize this dissolution of the marriage bond. Their main concern was to see that the *matrimonia initiata* were not broken up rashly, that a proper investigation as to the fact of nonconsummation was made, and that perjurers be brought to respect their original obligations which involved the indissolubility of their *matrimonium consummatum*.

d) *Peter Lombard*

Shortly after Gratian completed his great canonical synthesis, another Churchman of the same era, Peter Lombard (1100-1151), theologian of the School of Paris, completed his theological synthesis, the *Libri IV Sententiarum*.   We have seen the quite different attitude of this work to the question

---

[28] Cf. D'AVACK, *Cause*, pp. 428 and 449.
[29] HARRINGTON, "The Impediment of Impotency," p. 35.

of the formation of the marriage bond. Such a doctrine also revolutionized the attitude toward the problem of impotence.

After Peter Lombard, only two solutions for the problem of impotence are possible: one must either see impotence as a cause of nullity of marriage rather than a reason for divorce — or one must hold that impotence has no effect on the marriage bond and that marriages involving impotence are valid and indissoluble.[30] The latter was actually the solution adopted by the Church of Rome and is reflected in two Decretal letters that form part of the *Compilatio Prima antiqua*. Eventually, however, Rome itself was forced to be more realistic; it recognized the Gallican custom, and finally adopted it doctrinally.

Lombard himself opted for the first solution. Even though the distinction between a prohibiting and a diriment impediment had not yet been clearly established, he speaks of marriage being *irritum;* likewise he refers to the fact that force and fear *impede* consent.[31] Accordingly, he established categories of *personae plenae legitimae, penitus illegitimae* and *mediae legitimae;* he places the impotent person in the last category.[32] Hence he changes the whole approach to impotence; from a *vice, lack* or *defect* of the copula which makes the marriage, it becomes a *vice, lack* or *defect* which vitiates the act of consent by which marriage comes into being. Rather than a reason for divorce, it now becomes a diriment impediment.[33]

Such a shift in viewpoint also involves the perpetuity of impotence because the later is closely connected with the deeper questions which theologians and canonists are now forced to confront: why is impotence an impediment to marriage? how does it vitiate (annul) the effects of that moment of consent which forms a true marriage?

The history of the first faltering[34] attempts to answer this

---

[30] ESMEIN-GENESTAL, *Le mariage en droit canonique*, p. 266; D'AVACK, *Cause*, p. 430.

[31] LOMBARDUS, *Libri IV Sententiarum*, lib. IV, d. 30, p. 930.

[32] *Ibid.*, d. 34, p. 953.

[33] ESMEIN-GENESTAL, *Le mariage en droit canonique*, p. 259: "Ici, comme sur d'autres points, c'est veritablement une cause de divorce anciennement admise, qu'est changée en un empêchement dirimant."; D'AVACK, *Cause*, p. 431.

[34] HARRINGTON, "The Impediment of Impotency," p. 30: "There was a great deal of confusion in the 12th and 13th centuries as to whether or not the condition of impotency actually constituted an impediment to marriage, and if so, in what this impediment consisted."

question shows us that there were two types of response corresponding to the two questions raised. The more direct, and
in a sense superficial, indicated impotence was an impediment
to marriage because canon law made it one. This is what Lombard refers to when he speaks of the various types of *personae
legitimae*.[35] Later on St. Thomas, too, was to cite this reason
in explaining why impotence is an impediment to marriage:
"Tamen potest impotens esse tripliciter. Uno modo, quia non
potest *solvere de iure*. Et sic talis impotentia omnibus modis
facit contractum esse nullum ... "[36]

Yet Lombard did not hesitate to confront that even more
difficult question: how does impotence interfere with the formation of a valid marriage which takes place at the moment
of the exchange of consent of the parties? His explanation was
that the legitimacy of an impotent person was *media*, i.e. it depended on the knowledge and consent of the other contracting
party. If the other party knew about the impotence and consented to it, the marriage would be perfectly valid. On the
other hand, if the potent party were ignorant of the true situation, he would be considered to be in error. Hence, the
marriage would be invalid because he would not have given
his consent to a substantial modification (i.e. marriage without
sexual intercourse) of the usual marriage contract due to ignorance.[37] This explanation was seen to be quite valid and would

---

[35] LOMBARDUS, *Libri IV Sententiarum*, lib. IV, d. 34, p. 953: «Legitimae
iudicantur personae *secundum statuta patrum*, quae diversa sunt."
(Emphasis mine) Cf. ALBERT the Great, *Opera Omnia*, ed. A. Borgnet,
XXX: *Commentarium in IV Sent. D. 23-50* (Parisiis, 1894), d. 34, resp.,
p. 326: "Diffinitio [*sic*] tamen legitimae personae est, quae *secundum
leges* libertatem habet contrahendi matrimonium cum quocumque vo-
luerit." (Emphasis mine).

[36] THOMAS AQUINAS, *Supplementum Tertiae Partis Summae Theologicae*,
ed. Leonina (Romae: Marietti, 1956), q. 58, art. 1, ad 4um, p. 194.
(Emphasis mine).

[37] LOMBARDUS, *Libri IV Sententiarum*, lib. IV, d. 30, p. 930: "Nec solum
coactio impedit vel excludit consensum sed etiam *error*." (Emphasis
mine); Also, *ibid.*, d. 34, p. 953: "Si enim tales iunguntur *ignoranter...*";
(Emphasis mine); D'AVACK in *Cause*, p. 430, speaks of Lombard's idea
of the nullifying force of impotence: "Nel suo pensiero pertanto, più
che quale un incapacità personale del contraente impotente, *l'impotentia*
si presentava quale uno speciale caso di errore di qualità simile al-
l'*error servitutis*.); JOSEPH FREISEN, *Geschichte des canonischen Eherechts
bis zum Verfall der Glossentlitteratur* (Paderborn, 1893), p. 363. Also,
GERMAIN LESAGE, "Psychic Impotence: A Defect of Consent," *Studia
Canonica* 4 (1970), 64: "Peter Lombard based any request for nullity

play an important role henceforth in the thinking of theologians and canonists.[38]  However, it had its drawbacks and was
later replaced by an explanation of the nullifying force of impotence based on the maxim: *Nemo potest se obligare ad impossibile.*

### i) Perpetuity in Relation to Impotence as a Legal Impe-
diment

Until this point in history there had not been any explicit
mention of the requirement of perpetuity on the part of the
authors consulted.  From 1150 onwards, through the period of
the *Decretals of Gregory IX* and thence afterwards, we note
that authors are much more explicitly concerned to state that
*only perpetual* impotence invalidates a marriage.  Why?  It
seems that this realization gradually developed as the authors
reflected on the consequences of both the reasons (illegality
and ignorance) given to explain the nullifying force of impotence.

For even if one held that impotence was merely a *legal*
impediment, he would now become aware of the quite dispa-
rate juridical effects of perpetual as contrasted to temporary
impotence.

The authors of this period were familiar with the various

_____

due to impotence, on the fact that one of the contracting parties was
in error, since he ignored the other party's impotence."
    [38] Thomas Aquinas seems to adopt this position: "Ad primum ergo,
dicendum quod impedimenta illa quae sunt contra causam matrimonii,
vel contra essentiam ejus, impediunt matrimonium, secundum se, sive
sciantur, sive non; quae vero impediunt matrimonium ratione effectus
a quo coniuges possunt abstinere, si volunt, non impediunt matrimonium,
nisi quod generant alteri praeiudicium, cui non erit liberum uti matrimonio vel non uti: *Et huiusmodi sunt impotentia coëundi et conditio
servitutis*: Et ideo quando sciuntur matrimonium non impediunt; quia
hoc praeiudicium alter acceptat: ..." *Opera*, XI: *Commentarius posterior
super libros Sententiarum Petri Lombardi*, ed. Ioannis Nicolaus (Parisiis,
1660), dist. 36, q. 1, art. 1, 434.  (Emphasis mine).
    John Duns Scotus also briefly summarizes why the unknown im-
potence of the other party nullifies the contract: "Praeterea alia persona
[the potent party] intendit commutare potestatem sui corporis alterius;
ergo credit alium e converso posse commutare: sed non potest: ergo
hic est error pertinens ad aliquid, quod est per se requisitum ad contractum: talis autem error facit contractum nullum...." *Opera omnia*,
IX: *Quaestiones in lib. IV Sententiarum*, ed. cura Fr. Minorum Hibernorum Regularis Observantiae Collegii S. Isidori Romae cum commentario
Antonii Hiquaei (Lugduni, 1639), d. 34, q. 1, p. 728, n. 2.

forms of impotence: *frigiditas, castratio* in the male, *arctatio* in the female, and *maleficium* (impotence caused by a spell or curse).

The causes of the first three forms of impotence were biologically determined and absolute, i.e. they prevented one from engaging in intercourse with any other person. Such causes were easily discernible and could be proven by corporal inspection. These types of impotence also happened to be *perpetual.*

*Maleficium,* on the other hand, was caused by an indiscernible, generally transient force (a curse or spell). It was usually *temporary* and was not considered a serious condition.[39]

The authors of this period approached the dissolution of marriage as a question of nullity since they had adopted the viewpoint of the consent theory. Popes in the past seemed to have indicated different juridical consequences for natural impotence and for *maleficium* since they had given contrasting solutions to practical cases involving, respectively, natural impotence and *maleficium.* Hence, the authors could quite logically conclude that only *perpetual* impotence had the characteristics necessary to invalidate a marriage; for only the forms of *perpetual* impotence, based on *necessary* and *known* causes, constituted such serious personal incapacity as to interfere with the formation of marriage. Basing themselves simply on the decisions of decretal law, authors could hold that only perpetual impotence nullified.

*Maleficium* was understood to be a passing phenomenon, rather than a serious condition. The force of a curse or spell could be broken by a counter spell; prayer and penance were also able to banish the power of the devil; furthermore, no one could ever actually prove *maleficium* because it was not based on a necessary, observable cause.[40] For all these reasons it did not appear to fulfill the requirements necessary to annul the already given act of consent. Hence they concluded that *temporary* impotence does not invalidate marriage.

---

[39] *Glossa,* in C. 33, q. 1, c. 4, s.v. *nequibunt*: "...dixit Cardinalis quod iste finis non tenet, quia, ut dixit, nullum maleficium est perpetuum, quin saltem per ipsum auctorem tolli potest."

[40] This precise point of the provability of *maleficium* was to lead to a long controversy about whether such a spell was a sufficient reason to declare a marriage null. See Wernz-Vidal-Aguirre, *Ius matrimoniale,* p. 264, nota 15, for a summary of this point. Also see below, pp. 54-61.

Thus perpetual and temporary impotence gave rise to separate juridical consequences: perpetual impotence invalidated a marriage, temporary impotence did not.

### ii) Perpetuity in Relation to Impotence Seen as a Defect of Consent Due to Ignorance

The "ignorance" theory, also, and more logically, reaches the conclusion that *only perpetual* impotence nullifies. This theory, whose roots are found in Peter Lombard, holds that the basic flaw in a marriage involving impotence is a defect of consent. As a result of lack of knowledge about a fact substantially affecting the rights and obligation of the marriage contract, one partner (usually the potent party) has not freely consented.

How does the perpetuity or temporality of impotence make any difference with regard to the act of consent? Perpetuity or temporality makes a difference because of the way it would affect the presumptions ruling this act of consent.[41]

If *frigiditas* (perpetual impotence) were an existing problem before the act of consent (antecedent), and were not known to the potent party, he/she would be presumed not to have given his/her consent to this substantial modification of the marriage contract. Furthermore, the impotent party (in the case of easily discernible perpetual impotence such as *frigiditas*) would appear as one trying to deceive the other party by not informing him/her of a defect which should be known because based on a discernible natural cause such as malformation, disease, castration or narrowness of the vagina. The potent party would thus be presumed not to have given his consent for two reasons: 1) because there would be a substantial modification of the contract doing harm to him; 2) because of the likelihood of fraud on the part of the other party. The marriage would then be invalid because of his lack of proper consent. The validity of the marriage would really be dependent on the knowledge of the potent party contracting; if

---

[41] Anacletus Reiffenstuel points out the similar effect of error about the servile condition on the presumptions underlying the act of consent: "Ratio est quia error conditionis semper supponitur evacuare totum consensum.... merito praesumitur, nolle liberam personam commutare potestatem sui corporis cum potestate corporis servi, utpote quam non habet...," in *Ius canonicum universum*, IV, (Antwerpiae, ²1755), lib. IV, tit. 15, p. 98.

he knew and accepted the other's impotency, the marriage would stand.

In a situation of temporary impotence (*maleficium*), a quite different set of presumptions would come into play. The potent party would be presumed to have given his consent: first of all, because no one could impute an attempt at deception to the impotent party who could not in any way have known about this condition caused by an extrinsic evil influence; secondly, the transitory and ephemeral nature of the condition would not have been seen as a serious enough hardship to warrant the loved one's refusing to give his consent. Thus, in a case of *temporary* impotence, the marriage would be valid.

To sum up, the adoption of the consent theory brought a change in the relationship of impotence to marriage. It was no longer a cause for divorce, but an impediment to true matrimonial consent. As a result of reflecting on why impotence would interfere with consent, the authors were led to distinguish the different juridical requirements of temporary and perpetual impotence and to conclude that only the latter invalidates.[42]

The development spoken about above was not an immediate and clear reversal of fixed attitudes. Rather it was a halting gradual development flowing from the progressive consciousness of the notions of diriment impediment, and of the nullifying force of impotence. A continuation of our survey of some of the significant authors of the period between the *Decree of Gratian* (1140) *and the Decretals of Gregory IX* (1234) shows this.

### e) *Paucapalea and Rolandus Bandinelli*

Neither Peter Lombard, Paucapalea, nor Rolandus Bandinelli (Pope Alexander III - 1159-1181)[43] make any explicit mention of the need for the perpetuity of the impotence.

---

[42] Jean Dauvillier remarks on the change brought by the consent theory to the attitude towards impotence: "Elle devait être *perpétuelle* et *antécédente* au mariage, pour demeurer une cause de nullité et n'avoir pas le caractére d'un divorce, d'une rupture du lien." *Le mariage dans le droit classique de l'Eglise depuis le décrét de Gratien (1140) jusqu'à la mort de Clément V (1314)* (Paris, 1933), p. 180. (Emphasis mine).

[43] See PAUCAPALEA, *Summa*, ed. Johann Friedrich von Schulte (Giessen, 1890) (photo offset copy by Scientia Verlag, Aalen, 1965), C. 33,

## f) *Rufinus*

Rufinus (c. 1157) begins to recognize the different juridical consequence of impotence caused by *frigiditas* from that caused by *maleficium*.[44]

## g) *Stephen of Tournai*

Stephen of Tournai (1128-1203) speaks much more clearly of impotence as an impediment.[45] He refers to a dispute among authors as to whether *maleficium* was merely a reason for divorce, or whether it prevented marriage *ab initio*. He gives error as the reason why *maleficium* "impedit matrimonium contrahendum."[46] This very discussion shows a realization of the different juridical consequences of each and an attempt to establish principles concerning them. As yet, there is no requirement of perpetuity.

## h) *Bernard of Pavia*

Bernard of Pavia (c. 1191)[47] marks a new phase in the development of the canonical notion of impotence for two reasons: 1) He clearly sees it as a diriment impediment;[48] 2) and

---

pp. 130-134, and *Die Sentenzen Rolands nachmals Papstes Alexander III*, ed. A. Gietl (Freiburg im Briesgau, 1891).

[44] "Sciendum est itaque aliter se habere in frigiditate nature [*sic*], aliter in impossibilitate ex maleficio procedente." See *Die Summa Decretorum des Magister Rufinus*, ed Heinrich Singer (Paderborn, 1902), C. 33, q. 1, p. 497.

[45] "...quia quaedam sunt, quae impediunt contrahendum et dirimunt contractum, quaedam contrahendum impediunt, sed contractum non dirimunt." See *Die Summa des Stephanus Tornacensis über das Decretum Gratiani*, ed. Joh. Friedrich von Schulte (Giessen, 1891), C. 27, p. 231.

[46] *Ibid.*, p. 246. Cf. *also ibid.*, p. 239.

[47] *Bernardi Papiensis Summa decretalium*, ed. E. Laspeyres (Ratisbonae, 1860). This work was also called *Breviarium extravagantium*. It is a work of very great importance for two reasons: 1) It establishes the system of books and titles that all canon law will henceforth use; e.g. the subject of impotence will be found in the decretals and commentaries in lib. IV, tit. 15; 2) almost all later authors made use of this book either directly or indirectly. Cf A. VAN HOVE, *Prolegomena*, I (Mechlinae-Romae, ²1945), 447, n. 429.

[48] *Bernardi Papiensis Summa decretalium*, lib. IV, tit. 16, p. 176: "Frigiditas impedit matrimonium contrahendum et dirimit contractum... Maleficia etiam impediunt contrahendum et dirimunt post contractum...." Cf. also *ibid.*, lib. IV, tit., 1, p. 131. Thus A. Bride justly

reflecting more carefully on the problem of why impotence nullifies a marriage, he transfers it from the category of *defect of consent due to error* to an autonomous, independent cause of nullity, viz., a personal juridic *incapacity* based on a *defectus corporis*. Shifting from an exclusive concentration on the moment of consent, he declares that the marriage is null because of the fact that the impotent party cannot fulfill either of the purposes of marriage: procreation or the satisfaction of concupiscence.[49] Although he does not completely reject the former explanation,[50] by this statement, he directs canonical thinking on this matter into the path that it will henceforth pursue.

Once again a change of explanation has repercussions on the requirement of perpetuity; it makes of perpetuity a solid requisite for the impediment of impotence from that time onwards down to the present Code of Canon Law. For it is in connection with the ends of marriage that the perpetuity or temporality of impotence make a real difference. Temporary impotence says nothing about the validity or invalidity of marriage because there is at least the hope that the ends of marriage may, at some time in the future, be attained. Only perpetual impotence is a clear proof of the nullity of a marriage because it is only perpetual impotence that prevents the ends of marriage from *ever* being attained.

Bernard himself seems to have realized this since he stresses the idea of perpetuity: "... castratio et aliae infirmitates, quae reddunt *perpetuo* impotentem ad coeundum...." *Male-*

---

attributes to Bernard of Pavia the origin of our modern terminology on impediments in "Empêchements de mariage," *DDC*, V, col. 263.

[49] *Bernardi Papiensis Summa decretalium*, lib. IV, tit. 16, p. 175: " Inter alia matrimonia impedimenta impossibilitas coeundi maximum obtinet locum; cum enim matrimonium aut causa suscipiendae prolis aut causa incontinentiae fit, impossibilitas vero coeundi utramquae removet causam, restat, ut, ubi haec intervenerit, matrimonium excludatur."

Alexander III seems to use this same argument by the phrase: "Sicut enim puer qui non potest reddere debitum, non est aptus coniugio, sic quoque qui impotentes sunt minime apti ad contrahenda matrimonia reputantur." See X, IV, 15, 2.

[50] *Bernardi Papiensis Summa decretalium*, lib. IV, tit. 16, p. 180: «... quod si mulier, sciens virum impotentem, nihilominus acceperit eum, occasione impossibilitatis coeundi non poterit ab eo divortium postulare...." He may be speaking here of a merely procedural disability, which might not allow such a woman to bring a case to court. Cf. d'Avack, *Cause*, p. 445.

*ficium* for him is generally temporary, but *permanent* cases of it could exist.   Hence he recommends (as a criterion to distinguish permanent from temporary *maleficium*) the use of the *triennium experimentale* established by the Emperor Justinian to determine the time a couple must live together before indiscernible impotence could qualify them to receive a Roman civil divorce.[51]   After him, commentators will be careful to explicitly point out the requirement of perpetuity and they will begin to discuss the problems that flow from it.

### i) Innocent III

Innocent III (1198-1210) was to bring this whole process of development to a definitive conclusion in an authoritative decision as supreme lawgiver in the Church.   By this time the question, whether impotence was a diriment impediment or not, was no longer seriously in discussion.   He does not overlook the requirement of perpetuity, however.   Rather, he emphasizes it: in a Decretal Letter to the Bishop of Auxerre, in 1206, he recognizes that *only perpetual* impotence suffices for the diriment impediment. Furthermore, he goes on to define this notion of perpetuity: "...impedimentum illud non erat perpetuum, quod praeter divinum miraculum per opus humanum absque corporali periculo potuit removeri, ..."   This was to be the classic definition of the notion of perpetuity and the basis of all further comment.[52]

Innocent III does not give us any clue as to what he might have thought the nullifying force of impotence was; we can only surmise that he might have been familiar with the opinion of his contemporary, Bernard of Pavia.   His contribution to the story of the requirement of perpetuity is singular, for he is the one who authoritatively recognized and defined it.

This definitive contribution of Innocent III was the last development in the long process of understanding what was necessary to be able to declare that a particular case of impotence truly prevented a valid marriage. The dialogue between theology and canon law, the work of teachers and commentators, the solution of various practical cases — all had by this time led to broad agreement on what was to become the classic

---

[51] *Bernardi Papiensis Summa decretalium*, lib. IV. tit. 16, p. 177.
[52] X, IV, 15, c. 6.

doctrine. [53]    Within twenty years, all the progress made by the
commentators on the *Decree of Gratian* would be recapitulated
in the *Decretals of Gregory IX* (1234) and authentically promulgated as the law of the Church.    From then on authors would
be concerned not about the *requirement* of perpetuity, but
about the *meaning* of it as defined by Innocent III.


## 3. Conclusion

The purpose of this historical survey has been to discover
when the requirement of perpetuity was first introduced and
the reason for it.    It seems that we can definitely say that the
need for impotence to be perpetual was seen at the very time
it became clear that impotence was truly a diriment impediment rather than merely a legitimate reason for divorce.    This
development occurred in the last decades of the 12th century
and the first of the 13th, due to the growing acceptance at that
time of the consensual theory of the formation of the marriage
bond.

The requirement of the perpetuity of impotence became
part of the matrimonial law of the Church when it was included in the *Compilatio III antiqua* compiled by Peter of Benevento on the command of Innocent III.    This was authentically promulgated by the bull, *Devotioni vestrae* in the year 1210.[54]
By the later inclusion of this same Decretal Letter (*Fraternitatis tuae*) in the *Decretals of Gregory IX* (in lib. IV, tit. 15, c. 6),
the diriment impediment of impotence together with the requirement and definition of perpetuity became part of the common law of the Latin Church.[55]


## B. Reason for the Requirement of Perpetuity

The reasons for the requirement, or lack of it, vary in accord with one's understanding of the nature of the formation
of the marriage bond and of the nullifying force of impotence.

---

[53] Le Bras, "La doctrine du marriage," col. 2130: "L'affermissement
de la législation, le progrès des controverses permittront, au milieu du
XIII<sup>e</sup> siècle, l'achèvement d'une doctrine classique, presque unanime-
ment acceptée."

[54] Van Hove, *Prolegomena*, p. 356, n. 359.

[55] Oesterlé, "Impuissance," *DDC*, V, col. 1265.

For the adherents of the copula theory, only actual impotence which prevented consummation mattered; it was not really important whether this was perpetual or temporary because no truly indissoluble marriage bond had yet been created; the *matrimonium initiatum* could be dissolved for a legitimate reason such as this.

The relationship of impotence to the marriage bond is quite different when that bond is seen to have become indissoluble at the very time of consent of the parties. Impotence can only affect this bond if it is seen as having a nullifying force which vitiates and deprives of all value, the previous, apparently valid, act of consent. Two general explanations of the nullifying force of impotence (*capita nullitatis*) are given: *defectus consensus and incapacitas juridica (defectus corporis*). Both require that the impotence which nullifies be perpetual, but for different reasons.

The consent of the parties, which is the efficient cause of marriage, is essentially defective when one or both of the parties is ignorant of (in error about) a substantial modification of the marriage contract. All agree that a marriage without the possibility of the use of the right to sexual intercourse would be a substantially different kind of contract from the usual. Hence, ignorance or error about the fact of impotence could involve a vitiated act of consent, depending on whether or not the person would have consented, had he known of the impotence. And it is precisely here that the question of the perpetuity or temporality of the impotence makes a difference. For it is presumed that one would have consented in the case of temporary impotence, but would have refused if the impotence were perpetual.[56] Thus if the impotence is perpetual, the consent, and therefore the marriage, is invalid; if temporary, the consent and the marriage is valid.

---

[56] Cf. THOMAS SANCHEZ, *Disputationum de sancto matrimonii sacramento* (Antwerpiae, 1626), II, lib. 7, disp. 92, p. 334, n. 4. Here an argument is made that temporary impotence is not completely contrary to the purposes of marriage; it is not «...involuntarium simpliciter, sed secundum quid, instar error qualitatis." Such a phrase shows an analysis of the presumptions involved in the act of consent. Temporary impotence must be presumed to have been consented to. Therefore it does not nullify marriage. Perpetual impotence would be completely contrary to the ends of marriage. The presumption is that one would not have consented. Therefore, perpetual impotence nullifies.

Impotence can also be viewed as an autonomous and independent *caput nullitatis* as in C. 1068. Previously such a cause of nullity might have been termed *defectus corporis*, but it is now seen more as a *personalis incapacitas iuridica*.[57] For it *is* a *defect* of the *body*, a personal *incapacity* to fulfill either of the ends of marriage; procreation, or the mutual help and comfort characteristic of marital love (*remedium concupiscentiae*). An impotent person cannot make a valid contract to transfer the right to the use of his body for those acts suitable for propagation, if such a use is not in his own possession; if such does not, in fact, exist: *Nemo dat quod non habet.* Furthermore such a contract is invalid because the impotent person cannot oblige himself to an impossible obligation: *Nemo potest sese obligare ad impossibile.*

Thus we come to the reason for distinguishing the perpetual or temporary nature of the impotent condition. If the impotence is only temporary, the impotent person will at some time (therefore, at least *in spe*) be able to give over to the other party the actual use of sex, and so he may now validly contract about the right. Such is the case of the adolescent who has not yet reached full puberty. He will also be able to obligate himself because the fulfillment of the obligation will not be completely impossible for him. His temporary impotence does not interfere with his ability to contract a valid marriage.[58]

The situation is quite the opposite when the impotence is perpetual. The impotent person will never be able to participate in the use of sexual intercourse; he cannot transfer the right; he cannot obligate himself *sub gravi* to an impossible task. Thus this antecedent and *perpetual* impotence, whether on the part of the man or the woman, whether known to the other party or not, whether absolute or relative, invalidates marriage by the law of nature itself.

---

[57] d'AVACK, *Cause*, p. 440.

[58] SANCHEZ, *Disputationum de sancto matrimonii sacramento*, II, lib. 7, disp. 92, p. 333, n. 2. He states that perpetual impotence nullifies, but temporary impotence does not; he then gives the reason: "Et ratio utriusque partis ea est: quod perpetuae impotentiae repugnet obligatio ad copulam coniugalem ex matrimonii contractu consurgens. Impossibilium enim nulla potest esse obligatio. Secus de impotentia temporali. Quid enim in praesenti non est solvendo, cum tamen sit spes forte in futurum, potest ad solvendum obligari: cuius obligationis incapax est, qui numquam solvendo foret."

CHAPTER TWO

# TOWARDS THE RECOGNITION OF THE PERPETUITY OF IMPOTENCE AS A JURIDIC CONCEPT RATHER THAN A MERE FACT OF THE TEMPORAL-SPATIAL ORDER

### A. PROBLEMATIC: PERPETUITY, FACT OR CONCEPT?

The principal text concerning the perpetuity of impotence is Innocent III's Decretal Letter in reply to the Bishop of Auxerre, X, IV, 15, c. 6. A practical problem had been presented to Pope Innocent; his advice and a solution for this particular case were sought. The Bishop reported that a certain woman of his diocese had been married for a few years, but she and her husband were not able to consummate the marriage because of some defect of her genital organs.[1] The medical experts of the day (*matronae honestae*) had authoritatively declared her to be absolutely impotent.[2] The Bishop consequently dissolved the marriage on the basis of her impotence and permitted the man to remarry. Later on the same woman, now finding herself capable of sexual intercourse, entered a second marriage, with a certain Mr. G.

What must be done in this situation? Was the impediment of impotence present in this case? Must she return to her first husband? Was her first marriage a valid one?

Here we have the first presentation of the problem of the *mulier arcta* which was to be discussed and commented on for over six hundred years by most of the principal theologians and canonists.[3] The authors generally see two possible expla-

---

[1] "...cui naturale deerat instrumentum,.." X, IV, 15, c. 6.

[2] *Ibid.*: «...ut mulierem ipsam prudenter inspicerent, et perquirerent diligenter, utrum idonea esset ad viriles amplexus; quae tandem in fide sua tibi asseruere constanter, quod eadem mulier numquam poterat esse mater aut coniunx,...»

[3] The early decretalists who based their commentaries strictly on the texts of the *Decretals* tend to discuss varying principles for the solution of this same exact case. Later on, theologians commenting on

nations for such a problem: either the woman had a real natural defect of the vagina making sexual intercourse impossible, or at the least very difficult; or she was simply a virgin, but her husband was not able to penetrate her hymen due to its own natural toughness or some weakness on his part.

Innocent III's first reaction was to acknowledge the difficulty of the problem[4] and to deplore the lack of complete information. He was unsure whether to attribute the cure to medical means or to the simple fact of sexual intercourse with another man. Nonetheless he felt he had enough information to decide that the sentence of divorce issued by the Bishop was erroneous; she must return to her first husband, because, as a matter of fact,[5] her impediment was not perpetual and her first marriage was therefore valid:

> ...nos tamen, perspicaciter attendentes, quod impedimentum illud non erat perpetuum, quod praeter divinum miraculum per opus humanum absque corporali periculo potuit removeri, sententiam divortii per errorem, licet probabilem, novimus esse prolatam... et ideo inter ipsam mulierem et primum virum dicimus matrimonium extitisse.

By this decision he resolves the particular problem submitted to him. Furthermore, in the tradition of decretal law, he establishes this decision as a legal precedent which must be followed in resolving cases arising from either of the situations mentioned above.[6] Innocent III can, then, justly be regarded as the originator of the requirement of the perpetuity of im-

---

the *Sentences* of Peter Lombard, or canonists and moral theologians evolving their own syntheses, would discuss this same problem in a more general way. However, practically everyone who wrote about impotence discusses in one way or another the questions raised by this case.

[4] "De talibus autem non est facile iudicandum...." X, IV, 15, c. 6.

[5] *Ibid.*: "...quum pateat ex postfacto...."

[6] *Ibid.*: "Per haec autem quaestionem illam noveris esse solutam, qua quaeritur, utrum ea, quae adeo arcta est, ut nulli possit carnaliter commisceri, nisi per incisionem aut alio sibi modo violentia inferatur, non solummodo levis, sed forte tam gravis, ut ex ea mortis periculum timeatur, ad matrimonium contrahendum debeat idonea perhiberi. Similiter illa, quae viro, cui nupserat, adeo arcta est, ut numquam ab eo valeat deflorari, si ab eo sit per iudicium ecclesiae separata, et nubat alteri, cui arcta non sit, et per frequentem usum secundi reddatur etiam apta primo, utrum ad eum redire debeat, cum quo prius foedus inierat coniugale."

potence in ecclesiastical positive law because of this explicit legal precedent which he here recognizes as a paradigm for the solution of similar cases.

But the question immediately arises: What did he mean by those words: "...nos tamen perspicaciter attendentes, quod impedimentum illud, non erat perpetuum, quod praeter divinum miraculum per opus humanum absque corporali periculo potuit removeri..."? For at least two interpretations are possible.

The first, which we shall call the *factual* interpretation, stresses that the impotent condition which nullifies the marriage must in *fact*, in *reality*, be *perpetual*. Thus, if any time after the exchange of matrimonial consent, an impotent person should become potent, his marriage would be valid because his condition of impotency would not, in *fact*, have been perpetual. In such an interpretation, the word *perpetual* would be understood as requiring the physical condition of impotency to *actually* endure until the death of the one who has been declared impotent. According to such an interpretation, Innocent III's sentence on perpetuity would be translated as follows:

> Considering this case carefully, we conclude that *her* impediment was not perpetual, since it could be, *and as a matter of fact was, removed* by human means without any bodily risk or danger. Therefore the sentence declaring her absolutely and perpetually impotent was erroneous since she did, *in fact*, have sexual relations (at least with the second husband).

Contrast the above with the following alternate reading:

> Considering carefully the fact that *any such impediment which can be removed by human means without bodily risk is not perpetual*, we conclude that this sentence of divorce was erroneous. The facts show that she was able to have sexual relations without undue bodily risk; therefore the impotence does not qualify as perpetual; the first marriage is valid.

This second, or *conceptual*, interpretation would hold that Innocent III settles this particular case by establishing and defining a juridical *notion*, the perpetuity of the impediment of impotence. Perpetuity, then, would not be something of the purely physical, temporal-spatial order. Rather it would be a *concept*, an entity of the ethical and juridic order. In this view,

the perpetuity of impotence, just as the impediment of impotence itself, must not be seen as a merely physical fact which
can be measured in the time-space continuum; rather, it is a
principle of the moral order of rights and obligations.[7]  Accordingly in Chapter One we were able to explain the differing juridic consequences of perpetual and temporary impotence not
on the basis of duration of time, but on the possibility or impossibility of handing over a right.  In this view, perpetuity is
concerned primarily with the juridic determination of whether
a right or obligation could be transferred in a particular set of
factual circumstances rather than with the determination of
the actual duration of a physical, biological condition.  Perpetuity is a concept defining the principle one uses to determine
the effect on the validity of a marriage of the continuance or
the removal of a particular physical condition of impotence.
In short, the validity of the marriage does not depend on the
continuance or removal of the biological fact of impotence, but
rather on the ability or inability to morally, i.e. within the limits set by the concept of perpetuity, remove that biological
condition.  *Quod iure non possumus, id absolute non posse
censemur.*[8]  Hence only by understanding the text of Innocent III according to this *conceptual* interpretation can we
make sense of the statements that often appear among the later
authors to the effect that perpetuity is concerned more with
the *possibility* of removal rather than the actual removal of an
impotent condition.[9]

It is evident, then, that the meaning of perpetuity will vary
quite a great deal depending on whether we understand it as
a situation of fact or a concept of law.  We have seen that a

---

[7] Cf. KEATING, *Bearing of Mental Impairment*, p. 180:   "It is inaccu-
rate to define the impediment of impotence as the *physical* inability to
place *actus per se aptos ad prolis generationem;* it is rather the *moral*
inability to assume the right and obligation to place *actus per se aptos
ad prolis generationem.*" Also see J. FINNEGAN, "The Current Jurisprudence," p. 443; c. STAFFA 12 October 1951, *Dec.* 43, 626, n. 2.

[8] P. LAYMANN, *Theologia moralis* (Venetiis, 1719), lib. 5, tr. 10, pars
4, cap. 11, p. 383, n. 1.  Cf. also F. SCHMALZGRUEBER, *Ius ecclesiasticum universum,* IX (Romae, 1845), tom. IV, pars III, tit. 15, p. 152, n. 3.

[9] Salmanticenses (Theologians of Salamanca), *Cursus theologiae moralis Ff. discalceatorum B. Mariae de monte Carmeli collegii Salmanticensis,* II (Venetiis, ²1714), tom. II, tr. 9, c. 12, punc. 10, p. 161, n. 115:
"...quia perpetuitas impotentiae dirimens, non ex voluntate, sed ex
natura rei dependet, *neque attenditur, quod tollatur, vel non, sed quod
tolli possit....*" (Emphasis mine).

Rotal decision coram Sabattani on 10 April 1959 explicitly teaches that perpetuity is a juridic concept: "Perpetuitas impotentiae est conceptus iuris, non merus eventus facti."[10] d'Avack, too, holds that the perpetuity of impotence is a juridic concept.[11] Yet Antonio Vitale, in his article "La perpetuità dell'impotenza," written in rebuttal to the above decision c. Sabattani, presents a quite different view.[12] He disputes the basic premise that impotence is a *notio iuris;* for him it is merely a biological fact that happens to have juridic effects.[13] One cannot make a fact into a concept of law; perpetuity must be seen as the pure and simple time-dimension of a physical fact.[14] Only in such a way can we avoid decisions that go against logic and common sense such as one which would declare impotent a now fully capable man simply because his potency was regained by what was regarded, at the time of his marriage, as an extraordinary operation. In brief, he concludes that the Rota should return to the more rigorous, but more solid traditional criteria for judging the perpetuity of impotence.[15]

The precise purpose of this second chapter will be to investigate the meaning of perpetuity in its historical, traditional context. As such we will undoubtedly find references to perpetuity as a situation of fact, and as a juridic concept. Though

---

[10] c. SABATTANI, 10 April 1959, *ME* 84 (1959), 620, n. 5. Cf. also c. POMPEDDA, 19 June 1970, *ME* 96 (1971), 205, n. 5; c. PERSIANI, 15 November 1909, *Dec* 1, 140, n. 14.

[11] d'AVACK, *Cause*, p. 554: "Come s'intende, quindi, il concetto giuridico della perpetuità dell'impotenza resta pur sempre nel diritto matrimoniale canonico un concetto essenzialmente relativo e artificiale, distinto o, per lo meno, non sempre coincidente con quello fisiologico, nel senso che l'incapacità sessuale del soggetto si considera giuridicamente perpetua non solo quando la sua possibilità di scomparsa nell'avvenire sia da escludere in modo assoluto, ma anche quando essa risulti realizzabile e magari di fatto realizzata a determinate condizioni che il diritto considera antigiuridiche..."

[12] ANTONIO VITALE, "La perpetuità dell'impotenza," *IDE*, 73 (1962), 61-68.

[13] *Ibid.*, pp. 63-64: "Una cosa però è certa, e cioè che né il fatto, solo perché l'ordinamento giuridico esige che esso sia presente con determinate caratteristiche, perde la sua natura *di fatto* per diventare una nozione di diritto, né tanto meno queste determinate caratteristiche, solo perché l'ordinamento giuridico fa dipendere dallo loro presenza la relevanza giuridica del fatto si transformano esse stesse in concetti giuridici."

[14] *Ibid.*, p. 67.

[15] *Ibid.*, p. 68.

these positions might seem mutually exclusive, we must re-
member that each view is based on a variant perception of the
same reality. The impediment of impotence cannot be completely divorced from the physical condition of impotence; the impediment is rooted in this fact, but it is not completely coter-
minous with this physical fact. Perpetuity, too, is related to
the duration of this physical condition, but it too is something
more than this physical duration.

Hence in Chapter Two, as we seek to determine the meaning of perpetuity, we will do so in the light of the above controversy. Even though the authors make no explicit reference
to this distinction, we will try to deal with the matters that they
mention in a way that will help us to see whether perpetuity
is to be seen predominantly as a situation of fact or a juridic
concept. An answer is important for a true understanding of
perpetuity, especially as it might relate to areas outside the
strict limits of the impediment of impotence itself. If perpetuity predominantly involves the duration of a biological condition, then it becomes primarily a medical term. Perpetuity
will equal incurability, and will be determined by medical opinions and medical men. But if perpetuity is a juridic concept,
then the presence or absence of physical potency will be secondary to the legal reasoning and legal proofs used to show that
a particular situation fulfills the definition of perpetuity. If
perpetuity is a situation of fact, it will depend on the progress
of medical science; if it is a juridic concept, it will depend on
the growth and development of jurisprudence.

Furthermore, if it is a juridic concept, it will have to be
seen in relation to other concepts. We have already seen in
Chapter One how a new understanding of the formation of the
marriage bond had important repercussions on the concept of
diriment impediment. So, too, a more comprehensive insight
into the meaning of perpetuity could have repercussions in
areas outside the strictly defined limits of physical impotence.

B. BASIS FOR A REPLY: THE TEACHING OF PRINCIPAL
    CANONISTS AND THEOLOGIANS ON THE IMPEDIMENT
    OF IMPOTENCE, WITH SPECIAL EMPHASIS ON THE
    PERIOD 1200-1600

The period from 1200-1600 (roughly from the time of Innocent III to the Council of Trent) was a very rich one in the

history of Canon Law. This was the period of the formation of the *Corpus Iuris Canonici* during which the *Clementinae* and *Extravangantes* were added to the previous collections of the *Decretals*.[16] The system of decretal law, so characteristic of canon law, reached its zenith in the early part of this period. Decretal law was case law; it dealt with solutions to individual, concrete cases rather than establishing general solutions based on doctrinal, universal principles. The legislator established a precedent which had the force of law only in the particular case in question, but then became universally accepted through custom and perhaps later universal promulgation.

Canonical literature for the most part consisted in *Glossae*, which were commentaries written right in the margin of the text under discussion, or in *Commentaria*, autonomous commentaries on the *Decretals*. Only towards the end of this period did systematic works, which had little or no direct reference to the texts of the *Decretals*, appear.

At the same time a body of theological literature was being developed. The theologians, too, demonstrate the favor in which the exegetical method was held at this time; most of the great theological works produced during this era were commentaries on the *Sentences* of Peter Lombard.

Both theologians and canonists discussed the problem of impotence as an impediment to marriage; the former, in more general, universal terms; the latter, in relation to particular, individual cases.

What do they teach about the meaning of the perpetuity of impotence? In order to be able to answer that question we have to see the question in the context of the problems and controversies with which the authors themselves dealt. Our first task, then, will be to see how these authors understood the impediment of impotence itself.

---

[16] The Roman edition of the *Decretum Gratiani, Liber Extra, Liber Sextus, Clementinae, Extravagantes Ioannis XXII* and the *Extravagantes Communes* approved by Pope Gregory XIII in 1582 formed what is known as the *Corpus Iuris Canonici*. Cf. A. STICKLER, *Historia Iuris Canonici Latini*, I: *Historia Fontium* (Augustae Taurinorum, 1950), 273-275.

1. *The Impediment of Impotence Is Primarily Understood as*
*a Personal, Inhabilitating, Biological Male Defect*

Impotence is not a problem that affects the majority of
men. In fact, in her long history the Church has spent much
more of her energy in dealing with problems arising from
man's almost unlimited potentiality for sexual intercourse —
problems such as adultery, fornication, abortion and so forth.
Yet, problems of impotence did arise in the Middle Ages as
they had earlier in Roman times. Churchmen dealt with these
problems as they encountered them, in concrete particular
cases.

Accordingly, they described these situations in realistic,
rather than theoretical, terms: "non posse nubere," [17] "non possit coire," [18] "non posse operam carni dantes commisceri," [19]
"non potuit naturaliter concordare." [20] Hence their catch-all
term, *impossibilitas coëundi*, stressed the *actual* difficult situation; only later did the term, *impotentia coëundi*, which connotes the more abstract notion of potency, enter general usage.
As we have seen in Chapter One, this *impossibilitas coëundi*,
the inability to have sexual intercourse, had been recognized
quite early as something seriously interfering with marriage;
hence it was soon included in the category of an impediment
to marriage.

As one would expect, this concrete impossibility of sexual
relations was identified with its most prevalent cause, the natural physio-biological condition in the male known as *frigiditas*. Female impotence, as a real *impossibilitas coëundi*, was
practically unimaginable.[21]

---

[17] *Liber poenitentialis Teodori Cantuariensis*, lib. II, tit. 12, n. 33,
p. 330.

[18] C. 27, q. 2, c. 29.

[19] C. 33, q. 1, c. 2.

[20] *Ibid.*

[21] Cf. HOSTIENSIS (Henricus de Segusio), *Summa aurea* (Lugduni,
1568), lib. IV, tit. *de frigidis*, p. 315, n. 3: "Quia non potest esse uxor
quae apta non est ad viriles amplexus..."; THOMAS AQUINAS, *Supplementum Tertiae Partis Summae Theologicae*, q. 58, art. 1, ad 6um;
SANCHEZ, *Disputationum de sancto matrimonii sacramento*, II, lib. 7,
disp. 92, p. 333, n. 1: "Frigiditas enim reddens coniugem impotentem
soli viro accidit. Ut egregie docet D. Thomas ... quod mas fit agens in
generatione, femina vero solum patiatur. At frigiditas passioni non
obstat, sed soli actioni reprimens membri virilis motionem."

Frigidity was universally understood as something natural, something pertaining to the personal physical constitution of the individual.[22] Natural frigidity thus implied a biological condition which would prevent sexual intercourse absolutely, i.e. with anyone at any time.[23]

Since it arose from an intrinsic cause [24] and could not easily be remedied, it was generally regarded as something perpetual, something which would last until death.[25]

---

[22] C. 27, q. 2, c. 28: "...vir frigidae naturae..."; *Glossa ordinaria in Decretum Gratiani*, s. v. *naturaliter*; DOMINICUS SOTO, *In Quartum Sententiarum*, II (Venetiis, 1571), dist. 34, q. 1, art. 1, p. 238: "...frigiditas, eo quod a natura proficiscitur, quo utique nomine naturalis omnis impotentia coëundi denotatur."; *ibid.*, art. 2, p. 242: "Frigiditas, non accidentalis, quae transit, sed complexionis naturalis...."

[23] In his discussion of the signs of natural frigidity, Sanchez sums up the common teaching that natural frigidity is a biological condition. Cf. *Disputationum de sancto matrimonii sacramento*, II, lib. 7, disp. 94, p. 347, n. 5. For references which show that this biological condition absolutely prevents sexual intercourse, see the following: *Bernardi Papiensis Summa decretalium*, lib. IV, tit. 16, p. 176: "Frigiditas est quidam defectus naturalis caloris, *quo quis omnino a coitu impeditur.*" (Emphasis mine); *Glossa in Decretales*, s. v. *cognoscendi alios*; HOSTIENSIS, *Summa aurea*, lib. IV, tit. *de frigidis*, p. 315, n. 10: "...masculus iurabit se naturaliter frigidum, id est, *se non posse cognoscere aliquam mulierem, nec moveri ad voluntatem coëundi.* Nam si aliquoties moveretur et non possit perficere, non esset naturaliter frigidus." (Emphasis mine); HENRICUS HENRIQUEZ, *Summa theologiae moralis*, I (Venetiis, 1600), lib. 12, c. 7, p. 724, n. 5: "Sed frigiditas simpliciter etiam perpetua dicitur in viro, ea omnimoda et immendicabilis impotentia ad seminandum, *quae est ex qualitate intrinseca, et respectu omnium feminarum...*" (Emphasis mine); AUGUSTINUS BARBOSA, *Collectanea doctorum in ius pontificium universum*, II (Lugduni, ²1716), lib. IV, tit. 15, p. 556, n. 6: "Rursus impedimentum perpetuae impotentiae, aut esse potest *respectu omnium, prout est frigiditas,* similisve causa ad omnes quales...." (Emphasis mine).

[24] THOMAS AQUINAS, *Commentarius posterior super libros Sententiarum Petri Lombardi;* dist. 34, q. 1, art. 2, resp. p. 432: "...sive ex causa naturali intrinseca quae frigiditas appellatur..."; BONAVENTURA, *Opera theologica selecta,* ed. cura PP. Collegii S. Bonaventurae, Quaracchi, IV: *Liber IV Sententiarum* (Ad Claras Aquas - Florentiae, ²1949), dist. 34, art. 2, q. 1, ad 4um, p. 757: "Sed frigiditas quae est ex complexione et naturaliter inest,... haec est quae impedit, et haec est inseparabilis et perpetua."

[25] *Glossa ordinaria in Decretum,* s. v. *naturaliter*: "Naturaliter, id est, naturali frigiditate impediente. Et est argumentum quod *frigiditas est perpetuum impedimentum.*" (Emphasis mine); INNOCENT IV (Sinibaldus Fliscus), *Commentaria in V libros decretalium* (Venetiis, 1570), lib. IV, tit. 15, c. 2, p. 569: "...propter frigiditatem *vel alio perpetuo*

Because frigidity was perpetual, and the impediment of impotence was identified with frigidity, the *impediment* automatically began to be called perpetual; undoubtedly the authors understood this term in its new context in the way it had previously been applied to frigidity, that is, connoting a cause that biologically and absolutely prevented sexual intercourse. Thus the term "perpetual impediment," at least in the early part of this period, was more or less a shorthand abbreviation to indicate a naturally caused, stable, probably congenital (and therefore antecedent to any marriage) physical condition which prevented sexual intercourse. The contrary term, "temporary impediment," was consequently identified with the only common, natural physical type of temporary impotence — that due to age.[26]

In summary, an analysis of the principal texts on impotence shows that the authors of this period understood the *impediment* of impotence in very concrete terms. Because of their underlying presuppositions which we have tried to illustrate above, they identified the *impediment* with the physical condition, the personal bodily defect which physically prevented intercourse.[27] Such a narrow understanding of the im-

---

*impedimento*..." (Emphasis mine); HOSTIENSIS, *Summa aurea*, lib. IV, tit. *de frigidis*, n. 3: "Masculina vero naturalis impotentia — *frigiditas* — in homine *perpetua est*, et impedit matrimonium contrahendum, et dirimit iam contractum..." (Emphasis mine); RAYMOND of PENNAFORT, *Summa*, lib. IV, tit. 16, p. 513: "Naturalis impotentia in frigido, *quae est perpetua*, impedit matrimonium contrahendum, et dirimit iam contractum." (Emphasis mine); PANORMITANUS ABBAS (Nicolaus de Tudeschis), *Commentaria in libros decretalium*, VII (Venetiis, 1588), lib. IV, rubrica *de frigidis*, c. 4, p. 60, n. 5: "...nam saepe dubitabitur, utrum frigiditas sit *naturalis*, et *perpetua*, an *accidentalis*, et *temporalis*,..." (Emphasis mine).

[26] RAYMOND of PENNAFORT, *Summa*, lib. IV, tit. 16, p. 513: "Naturalis, et temporalis, quae est in puero,..."; HOSTIENSIS, *Summa aurea*, lib. IV, tit. *de frigidis*, n. 3: "Naturalis impotentia communis utriusque sexus est temporalis, nam adveniente pubertate expirat."

[27] PANORMITANUS, *Commentaria in libros decretalium*, VII, lib. IV, rubrica *de frigidis*, c. 6 p. 60 n. 6: "Item nota hic regulam satis notandum in materia matrimoniali: quod *omne impedimentum viri, vel mulieris,*... reddit quem *inhabilem* ad contrahendum..." (Emphasis mine); ANTONIUS a BUTRIO, *In libros decretalium commentarii*, IV (Venetiis, 1578), lib. IV, tit. 15, c. 2, p. 39, n. 5: "Quidam sunt *impediti frigiditate,*... Quidam sunt *impediti maleficio*..." (Emphasis mine); *ibid.*, c. 6, p. 40, n. 5: "Nota quarto — quia articulus debet concludere mulierem indiffinite *inhabilem* quo ad omnes, et quo ad omne tempus, ita

pediment of impotence was to give rise to many doubts, hesitations and controversies; through a process of gradual development culminating in the work of Soto and Sanchez, the controversies were settled, the presuppositions overcome, and the notion of the impediment of impotence broadened.

## 2. Controversies Which Led to a Broader, Conceptual Understanding of the Impediment of Impotence

The concrete, biological understanding of the impediment of impotence is a constant element in the literature on impotence and the perpetuity of impotence. However, there was also a slow process of development toward a broader understanding of impediment, largely brought about by the discussion of two serious problems, that of the *mulier arcta* and that of *maleficium*. The scholarly debate led to general agreement by the early part of the seventeeth century on two principal conclusions: 1) natural respective impotence formed part of the impediment of impotence; 2) accidental relative impotence also formed part of the impediment of impotence. These conclusions logically forced an attenuation and abandonment of the concrete, biological understanding of the impediment of impotence. As a result, the impediment, understood in a much broader sense, was able to be recognized, itself, as a general principle of the juridic order, a juridic entity. Consequently, the perpetuity of impotence could also be understood in a broader sense as a juridic concept rather than a merely physical fact.

### a) The Case of the "Mulier Arcta": Acceptance of Natural Respective Impotence, a Victory over the Biologically Absolute Understanding of the Impediment of Impotence

In the context of this concrete biological notion of the impediment of impotence, we can understand why the particular case referred to Pope Innocent III in X, IV, 15 c. 6 caused such a knotty problem. First of all, the case deals with the problem of impotency in a woman; secondly, after she was judged im-

---

quod non potest esse mater, vel coniunx aliquo tempore." (Emphasis mine).

4

potent and the marriage dissolved, she was found to be *in fact*
capable of sexual intercourse.

Many questions could be raised and were raised by the
commentators and glossators down through the years; the principal one seemed to be that posed to Innocent: Must the first
marriage be re-established? This, of course, involves the question: Is the first marriage the valid one? In turn, one must
ask: Was the first marriage nullified by the diriment impediment of impotence? All these questions essentially involve the
basic one: Is the problem of *arctatio*, a natural defect of the
female which interferes with sexual intercourse, included in
the notion of the impediment of impotence?

As we might expect, the first responses to this question
were quite negative. Pope Innocent III decided that the first
marriage was valid; that there was no impediment in this case.
His reasoning seems to be: the only *real impediment* of impotence is a perpetual one, — a permanent, absolutely biological
defect which prevents intercourse with anyone at any time.
Consequently this case cannot be considered to fall under the
category of the impediment of impotence because: 1) it involves impotence on the part of the woman, and there can be no
permanent biological impediment in women; [28] 2) the impediment in this case is not absolute, since the woman has *in fact*
engaged in sexual relations.[29]

The *Glossa ordinaria on the Decretals* (completed about
1263) likewise reflects the opinion that there can be no impediment here because subsequent sexual relations have taken
place.[30] The Glossators also note the unusual biological cause
which is asserted in this case.[31]

---

[28] See footnote 21 of this chapter.

[29] X, IV, 15, c. 6: "Contigit autem postea quod mulier eadem invenit
qui seras huiusmodi reseravit,...", "...quum pateat ex postfacto, quod
ipsa cognoscibilis erat...."

[30] The *Glossa on the Decretals* is found in the following edition of
the *Decretals*: *Decretales Gregorii IX una cum glossis*, editio ad exemplar Romanum (Venetiis, 1604). The *Glossa* very strongly maintains
that any subsequent sexual experience will indicate that the woman
must be returned to her first husband. Even if this first marriage
should be dissolved on the basis of the same impotence a second, third
or infinite number of times, she still must be returned to her first
husband every time that experience proves her capable of sexual intercourse. Cf. *ibid.*, c. 6, s. v. *fornicario modo*: "Quia nescitur an sit apta
viro primo: et hoc aliquo iure perpendi non potest, sed potius per ex-
perientiam." The basis of this position is indicated in *ibid.*, c. 7 s. v.

Pope Innocent IV (Sinibaldo Fieschi † 1254) in the clearest possible terms and without any equivocation whatsoever holds that the first marriage of the *mulier arcta* is valid because the impediment in this case was not biologically absolute:

> ...melius placet... primo semper restituenda est... quia si mulier est arcta uni, omnibus arcta est, et si uni est cognoscibilis, et omnibus est cognoscibilis. Item si aliquando est cognoscibilis, non habet neque naturale, neque perpetuum impedimentum...[32]

He summarily dismisses possible explanations which tried to reconcile the reality of the impediment with the fact of subsequent sexual intercourse.[33] His solution for this case is based on one clear principle: the woman was perfectly suited for the first marriage because she did not have a perpetual (i.e. biologically absolute) impediment.[34]

The necessity for the impediment to be perpetual (understood in the above sense) was common teaching for at least two hundred years and was espoused by the following authors: Henry of Susa, Cardinal-Bishop of Ostia († 1271) who is better

---

*cognoscendi alios*: "...quia si quis est frigidus quo ad unum, quo ad omnes est frigidus, cum impedimentum a natura procedit." The only case in which the Glossators would permit permanent separation from the first husband would be that involving physical danger to her from the attempts at consummation. See below for further discussion of this aspect.

[31] *Ibid.*, c. 3 s. v. *a natura*: "...quia erat arcta, ut dixi." *Ibid.*, c. 6 s. v. *divinum miraculum.*

[32] INNOCENT IV, *Commentaria in V libros decretalium*, lib. IV, tit. 15, c. 6, p. 569, n. 1; also *ibid.*, p. 571, n. 7.

[33] Some authors (Goffredus, according to Hostiensis) had offered the explanation that a physical disproportion of genital organs could constitute the impediment of impotence for a particular couple. In other words, respective, rather than absolute, impotence could constitute the impediment.

Innocent IV dismisses such a theory in *ibid.*, c. 6, p. 569, n. 1: "...melius placet quod ...sive per concubitum alterius viri etiam dissimilis in genitalibus reddatur apta, primo semper restituenda est..."; see also *ibid.*, p. 571, n. 7.

[34] Cf. *ibid.*: "...plus placet [opinio] quod idonea sit quia perpetuum impedimentum non habet, unde dicimus quod separata a viro propter arctationem si incidatur etiam cum periculo, tamen priori viro restituenda est...."

known under the name Hostiensis; [35] Thomas Aquinas (1226-
1274); [36] Raymond of Pennafort († 1275); [37] Ricardus de Mediavilla (Richard of Middleton † 1308); [38] Durandus a Sancto Porciano († 1332); [39] Ioannis Andreae (1270-1348).[40]

Panormitanus (1386-1453) appears to be the first author
who dares to disagree with the concrete decision that the *mulier arcta* must be returned to her first husband.[41] In effect, he
holds that a case of *arctatio*, the natural biological impotence
of the female, can constitute a form of the impediment of impotence. [42]   He reaches this conclusion by first obliquely under-

---

[35] HOSTIENSIS, *Summa aurea*, lib. IV, tit. de frigidis, p. 317, n. 16:
"...quia nunc apparet quod impedimentum fuit temporale, quod ex
post facto cessavit, sed nullum temporale impedimentum matrimonium
dirimit, secundum omnes."

[36] THOMAS AQUINAS, *Supplementum Tertiae Partis Summae Thelogi-
cae*, q. 58, art. 1, resp.: " Unde, si Ecclesia se deceptam inveniat, per
hoc quod ille in quo erat impedimentum, invenitur carnalem copulam
cum alia vel cum eadem perfecisse, reintegrat matrimonium praecedens, et dirimit secundum, quamvis de eius licentia sit factum."

[37] RAYMOND of PENNAFORT, *Summa*, lib. IV, tit. 16, p. 513, n. 1.

[38] RICARDUS DE MEDIAVILLA, *Super quatuor libros Sententiarum*, IV
(Brixiae, 1591), dist. 34, art. 2, q. 1, p. 476: "...quia tunc constabit ecclesiam fuisse deceptam in iudicando impedimentum perpetuum quod
erat temporale."

[39] DURANDUS A SANCTO PORCIANO, *Petri Lombardi Sententias theologicas
commentariorum libri IV* (Vol. II of the photo offset edition by the
Gregg Press, Inc., Ridgewood, N. J., 1964) (Venetiis, 1571), dist. 34 q. 2,
p. 380, n.7: "...quia constat ecclesiam fuisse deceptam in iudicando
perpetuum impedimentum quod fuit temporale...."

[40] IOANNIS ANDREAE, *In IV decretalium librum novella commentaria*,
IV (Venetiis, 1581), lib. IV, tit. 15, c. 6, p. 51, n. 29: " ...quia nunc
praesumitur quod fuit impedimentum temporale...."

[41] PANORMITANUS, *Commentaria in libros decretalium*, lib. IV, rubrica *de frigidis*, c. 6, p. 61, n. 19: «...tunc puto quod non sit restituenda
primo, licet per frequentem usum cum secundo sit reddita apta primo...."

[42] *Ibid.*, p. 57, introduction.  Here Panormitanus explains that the
title of this section of the *Decretals* is called: "de frigidis et maleficiatis et de impotentia coëundi."  The reason for the third term is specifically to include cases such as *sectio* (and by analogy *arctatio*) which
do no strictly come under either of the previously recognized forms of
impotence.  In *ibid.*, p. 60, n. 6, he admits that the impediment can
exist also in the female: "...impedimentum viri, vel mulieris...."
Later authors also recognize that the term *impotentia coëundi* is wider
than mere frigidity; nevertheless they would allow the term *frigiditas*
to be a general designation for any type of natural impotence. Cf. SOTO,
*In Quartum Sententiarum*, II, dist. 34, q. 1, art. 1, p. 238, introduction:

mining the biological basis of the impediment; he allows one to claim impotence, even though one may not be able to indicate an evident natural cause.[43]  Furthermore he explicitly attacks the presumption that impotence is necessarily absolute by rejecting Innocent IV's axiom: "cognoscibilis uni, cognoscibilis omnibus." [44] A situation can exist in which there would be a true impossibility for sexual relations between a particular man and woman, even though each may be capable of sexual relations with someone else.[45]  Such a condition is defined as natural respective impotence, and Panormitanus is one of the first to conclude that the natural respective impotence called *arctatio* constitutes a form of the impediment of impotence.[46]

Other authors show similar reasoning processes in attempting to resolve the case of the *mulier arcta*, although they do not dare to contradict the decision given by Innocent III.  Hostiensis seems prepared to accept respective impotence in theory, but has serious questions about it and would like a further papal decision on the matter.[47]

Ioannis Andreae notes that one should not worry about the cause of the impotence; as long as the person is truly impotent, the impediment will exist.  Thus even respective natural impotence, *arctatio*, constitutes the impediment.[48]

---

"...frigiditas, eo quod a natura proficiscitur, quo utique nomine naturalis omnis impotentia coëundi denotatur."

[43] PANORMITANUS, *Commentaria in libros decretalium*, VII, lib. IV, rubrica *de frigidis*, c. 2, p. 58, n. 3: "...quod sufficit allegare viri impotentiam absque eo, quod specificetur qualitas impotentiae."

[44] *Ibid.*, p. 60, n. 7: "...si mulier est cognita ab un viro, praesumitur quod sit cognoscibilis a quolibet viro: puto tamen quod haec praesumptio recipiat probationem in contrarium, ut patebit ex inferis dicendis."

[45] E.g. *ibid.*, p. 61, n. 19, in the case of a disproportion of genital organs.  Panormitanus had already admitted the existence of relative impotence as a solution to the problem of *maleficium*, cf. *ibid.*, c. 1, p. 58, n. 7. Further reflection on this probably led him to also assert relative impotence in the case of *arctatio*.

[46] John Duns Scotus had apparently also reached the conclusion, at least in theory, that respective natural impotence could exist and could constitute the impediment of impotence: "...sed etiam naturale impedimentum potest esse respectu unius personae, et non respectu alterius, maxime de naturali in muliere." Cf. *Quaestiones in lib. IV Sententiarum*, dist. 34, q. 1, p. 730, n. 5.

[47] HOSTIENSIS, *Summa aurea*, lib. IV, tit. *de frigidis*, p. 317, n. 16.

[48] IOANNIS ANDREAE, *In IV decretalium librum novella commentaria*, IV, lib. IV, tit. 15, c. 4, p. 48:  " Unde non curo, qualiter sit impotens,

It was through the influence of Didacus Covarruvias a Leyva (1512-1577), Bishop of Segovia, that natural respective impotence was definitively recognized as constituting a form of the impediment of impotence. He was given a special papal mandate to decide a difficult marriage case involving a virgin bride whose spouse was so weak that he could not consummate the marriage.[49] Bishop Covarruvias decided that this natural respective impotence constituted a form of the impediment of impotence. By this decision and its acceptance as common teaching, the narrow biologically absolute understanding of the impediment of impotence was definitively overcome.[50] A new phase in the understanding of the impediment of impotence was to follow shortly.

### b) *The Problem of "Maleficium": Acceptance of Relative Impotence Without Any Biological Basis as a Form of the Impediment*

The second, and even more important question dealt with by the authors of this period concerned the problem of a form of impotence that was completely relative and had no biological or physical basis whatsoever. The controvery concerned *maleficium*, impotence caused by the influence of the devil and brought about by an evil spell. The point in dispute was: Could such a form of impotence be perpetual?

To the modern reader, the fascination of medieval authors with *maleficium*, impotence supposedly caused by an evil spell,

---

sive propter arctationem sive propter aliam causam: quia si postea contrahit, non tenet matrimonium, ex eo quo non potest adiuvari...."

[49] D. COVARRUVIAS a LEYVA, *Opera omnia*, II (Lugduni, 1661), *Tractatus de frigidis et maleficiatis et impotentia coëundi*, q. 1, p. 535: "...*coactus tamen Sanctae Sedis delegatione* causae cuiusdam gravis profecto, *et quae mihi molesta fuit*, non potui non hac de re aliquot quaestiones ac dubia tractare, quae apud iuris utriusque interpretes variis sententiis et opinionibus sic explicentur, ut omnino sit necesse, quid iure tenendum aut respondendum, et deliberate maturius et cautius definire." (Emphasis mine).

[50] Shortly after Covarruvias' landmark decision, his fellow Spaniard, Thomas Sanchez, conclusively demonstrated how such natural respective impotence can be reconciled with the text of the *Decretals* and can constitute the impediment. Cf. SANCHEZ, *Disputationum de sancto matrimonii sacramento*, II, lib. 7, disp. 93, p. 340, n. 5. This opinion soon became common teaching by the strength of his argumentation and the weight of his authority.

seems strange and superstitious. We wonder why so many canonists and theologians devoted so much time and energy to discussing what should have been a very rare phenomenon. Yet, the controversy over *maleficium* was merely a symptom of the deeper struggle over the true meaning of the impediment of impotence. The general consensus finally reached accepting *maleficium* as a form of the impediment had a twofold effect: it was the deathblow for the previous physio-biological understanding of the impediment and the impetus for the conceptual understanding of the impediment. As a necessary consequence, the perpetuity of the impediment was also able to be recognized as a concept in its own right.

Thomas Sanchez gives us a detailed resumé of the early teaching on *maleficium* in II, lib. 7, disp. 94 of his tractatus *Disputationum de sancto matrimonii sacramento.* There can be no doubt that such impotence brought about by a curse or spell truly exists. The devil is able to accomplish this in five principal ways. Such impotence can affect women as well as men. *Maleficium* can be distinguished from frigidity by several signs. The principal differences, however, are that *maleficium* can be relative, and it is not based on a natural cause.[51]

*Maleficium* usually affects sexual relations with one person only. This is possible because it does not depend on a necessary, determined cause such as a natural defect.[52] Precisely because no natural obstacle can account for the impossibility of intercourse in this case, one must attribute the cause to the influence of the devil.[53]

From this brief summary of the teaching on *maleficium* we immediately note that *maleficium* directly contradicts the widely held basic presuppositions about impotence that we had seen earlier: for it is neither absolute, nor biologically determined.

The most disputed point in the controversy over *maleficium* was whether or not it could be perpetual. As we have seen above, the word "perpetual" in the context of this discussion was a sort of abbreviation for absolute and biologically determined. The emphatic force of the question is not on perpetual as a

---

[51] *Ibid.,* disp. 94, pp. 346-348, nn. 1-6.

[52] *Ibid.,* p. 347, n. 4: "...quia diabolus voluntarie et non *ex naturae necessitate agat,* potest respectu unius impedire, relicta potentia non impedita erga alias personas." (Emphasis mine).

[53] *Ibid.,* p. 348, n. 6: "Cum enim tunc nullum obstaculum naturale dari possit, tribuendum est daemoni impedienti congressum..."

duration of time, but as connoting absolute and biologically determined. Therefore the question: can *maleficium* be perpetual? must really be interpreted: can such a relative, undetermined type of impotence really constitute the impediment of impotence?

It would seem that there really should be no controversy on this point. In accord with the general teaching on the impediment, the response should be quite simple and direct:

Major:      the impediment of impotence is always biologically determined (perpetual).

Minor:      impotence due to *maleficium* is never perpetual (biologically determined).

Conclusion: therefore impotence due to *maleficium* never constitutes the impediment of impotence.

However, this clear logical position was untenable: the *Decree of Gratian* and the recent *Decretals of Gregory IX* clearly admitted that *maleficium* could nullify a marriage, could constitute a form of the impediment of impotence.

Gratian had included the section "... si per sortiarias" of Hincmar of Rheims in C. 33, q. 1, c. 4. Thus he clearly provided a basis for granting separations and allowing *both* parties to remarry in a case of impotence due to *maleficium*. However, his laconic comment post c. 4 noting the conflict between this canon 4 and the previous canon 2 of Gregory seems to indicate some doubt over the wisdom of Hincmar's decision:

> Sed in hoc videtur contrarius premisso capitulo Gregorii. Ibi secundo nupserat, et redire ad primum. Hic autem vivente eo, cui secundo copulata fuerat, primo reconciliari non poterit.

The *Decretals of Gregory IX* only deepened the confusion. On the one hand, they provided examples of new cases solved according to the basic principles: X, IV, 15, c. 5 (*Laudabilem*) grants an annulment on the basis of impotence, but then says this must be rescinded if the impotent party marries again. The clear deduction from this is that impotence must be absolute and biologically determined; if the person declared impotent is found capable then the annulment must be rescinded because his impotence was not absolute and biologically determined.

Yet at the same time the *Decretals* provided a solution almost exactly parallel to that of Hincmar contained in C. 33, q. 1, c. 4.

Chapter 7 (*Litterae vestrae*) of X, IV, 15 allowed a man who suffered from a form of impotence that was neither absolute nor biologically determined to be declared impotent;[54] it officially declared that a relative and biologically undetermined form of impotence could constitute the impediment.

Thus the early commentators were faced with two options: either deny that *maleficium* could constitute a form of the impediment, or change their basic presupposition that the impediment of impotence must be something absolute and biologically determined. The latter choice, at first, was not something possible for them because they had not yet consciously reflected on this possibility. Accordingly, their first gut reaction is to deny that *maleficium* could be a form of the impediment, could be perpetual.

The *Glossa ordinaria in Decretum* records the opinion of one of the early commentators that no authority should be given to C. 33, q. 1, c. 4, since this was not the decision of a pope, but merely of the Archbishop of Rheims. The commentator does not think much of the intellectual ability of Hincmar; he says he should be called "ignarus" rather than Gnarus. Everyone knows that no *maleficium* can be perpetual.[55]

Innocent IV, who in 1251 composed one of the earliest commentaries on the *Decretals*, implies that *maleficium* does not constitute the impediment when he forcefully declares that no marriage should be broken up on account of *maleficium*.[56] He refuses to accept the view that c. 7 (*Litterae vestrae*) concerns a case of *maleficium*: rather than destroy his presupposition that the impediment must be absolute and biologically determined, he prefers to conclude that the person alleging such a nebulous form of impotence is a liar.[57]

---

[54] X, IV, 15, c. 7, grants an annulment ("...proferatis divortii sententiam inter eos.") to a man who does not have absolute ("...sed tamen se habere potestatem cognoscendi alias asserebat.") impotence.

[55] *Glossa ordinaria in Decretum* in C. 33, q. 1, c. 4 s. v. *nequibunt*. The commentator is called Cardinal and is probably the early commentator known as Cardinalis Gratianus. At the time of composition of his *Glossa in Decretum* (1160), c. 4 was attributed to " Gnarus " which is an evident corruption of " Hincmarus ".

[56] INNOCENT IV, *Commentaria in V libros decretatium*, lib. IV, tit. 15, c. 5, p. 569: " Nos dicimus quod propter maleficium, numquam separatur matrimonium...."

[57] *Ibid.*, c. 7, p. 571, n. 1: " ...quia licet ipse diceret se habere potentiam cognoscendi aliam, non creditur sibi, nec verum erat."

The *Glossa ordinaria in Decretales* (completed 1263) takes a first hesitating step away from this firm denial of *maleficium* as a form of the impediment, by offering an interpretation of Hincmar's canon that can be reconciled with the prevailing biological presupposition.[58] Moreover, the Glossa even admits the theoretical possibility of relative impotence.[59]

Hostiensis (+1271), too, shows a growing tendency to move away from the strong position advocated by Innocent IV. He is familiar with the arguments that Hincmar's canon (*Si per sortiarias*) should be abandoned, but does not agree with them. He seems to be saying: perhaps *maleficium* can be admitted as a form of the impediment, even though it is not absolute or biologically determined.[60] In this context, he cites the reason given by Goffredus to explain the nullifying force of *maleficium*: like any other form of *impossibilitas coëundi*, it directly vitiates both ends of marriage, the procreation of offspring and the avoidance of fornication.[61]

Here we see the beginning of a whole new approach to the question whether *maleficium* can be a form of the impediment. From here on some authors will begin to consider, though perhaps not yet reflexively, the other option which would solve the dilemma caused by the problem of *maleficium*. Instead of denying a conclusion recognized by the authority of the law itself, i.e. *maleficium* does constitute a form of the impediment of impotence, they seem to have revised their major premise, their basic presupposition. This new mode of reasoning may be illustrated as follows:

> Major:    the impediment of impotence, rather than being something always absolute and biologically determined, is always something which prevents the ends of marriage from being attained.

---

[58] *Glossa ordinaria in Decretales* in X, IV, 15, c. 6 s. v. *divinum miraculum*.

[59] *Ibid.*, c. 7 s. v. *cognoscendi alios*: "...quia si quis est *frigidus quo ad unam, quo ad omnes est frigidus,* cum impedimentum a natura procedat — *secus* in maleficiato." (Emphasis mine).

[60] HOSTIENSIS, *Summa aurea*, lib. IV, tit. de frigidis, p. 316, n. 8: "Item *aliquando* maleficiatur homo adeo quod non potest cognoscere uxorem suam sed bene cognoscit omnes alias." (Emphasis mine).

[61] *Ibid.*, n. 9.

Minor:            *maleficium* is something which prevents the
                  ends of marriage from being attained.

Conclusion:       therefore, *maleficium* is a form of the impedi-
                  ment of impotence.

Such a change in viewpoint did not come about consciously
or rapidly; it was part of a slow process of growth and development of the idea of the impediment of impotence, fostered
mainly by the great Scholastic theologians.     Jurists, such as
Ioannis Andreae, Antonius a Butrio and Panormitanus, since they
were more concerned with individual cases and had to hold
more closely to the authoritative texts, only grudgingly and
slowly began to admit that *maleficium* could be perpetual and
could constitute a form of the impediment.[62]

Panormitanus provides us with an example of the tenacity
with which the biological presupposition still maintained its
hold; he finds it possible to admit *maleficium* as perpetual if the
curse is given in food and drink and thus works on the victim
through the influence of these natural forces.[63]

St. Bonaventure (1221-1274) is one of the first authors to
illustrate this subtle shift in the notion of the impediment of
impotence.  He recognized that impotence is primarily a natural
defect,[64] but he distinguished between forms of impotence which
*inseparably* and *perpetually* impeded and those which did not.[65]

---

[62] IOANNIS ANDREAE, *In IV decretalium librum novella commentaria*,
IV, lib. IV, tit. 15, c. 7, p. 51, n. 16. ANTONIUS a BUTRIO, *In libros decretalium commentarii*, VI, lib. IV, tit. 15, c. 6, p. 41, n. 20: "...quia *potest
est* quod sit maleficiatus quo ad unum et non quo ad alium, quia talia
*impedimenta* sunt quo ad personam certam restrictibilia." (Emphasis
mine).

[63] PANORMITANUS, *Commentaria in libros decretalium*, VII, lib. IV,
rubrica *de frigidis*, c. 6, p. 60, n. 15: "...nam saepe ista impedimenta
(maleficia) sunt perpetua, unde quum mortuus est ille qui fecit, vel
maleficium est perditum, vel *si fuit datum in potu vel cibo*." (Emphasis mine); cf. also SYLVESTER PRIERAS (Silvester Mazolini), *Summa Sylvestrina*, II (Venetiis, ²1581), Pars 2a, s. v. *matrimonium*, VIII, p. 167:
"Potest autem maleficium praestare impedimentum quantum ad omnes, et quantum ad unam tantum: quia diabolus est causa voluntaria,
non ex necessitate naturae agens.  Sed intellige, *nisi utatur activis na-
turalibus*." (Emphasis mine).

[64] BONAVENTURA, *Liber IV Sententiarum*, dist. 34, *divisio textus*, p.
752: « Primo enim agit de impotentia coëundi, quae respicit defectum
naturae."

[65] *Ibid.*, art. 2, q. 1, ad 4um, p. 757: "...frigiditas duplex est: quaedam accidentaliter, quaedam complexionaliter et per naturam.  Illa quae
est in homine accidentaliter, potest ut plurimum expelli, pro eo quod

For him, *maleficium* was not biologically absolute,[66] yet it was truly an impediment to marriage.[67] The reason he gives to show why it qualifies as an impediment illustrates the shift from a purely physical to conceptual idea of the impediment: *maleficium* interferes with the rendering of the marriage debt in exactly the same way as *frigiditas* or *arctitudo*, therefore, it, too, must be an impediment to marriage.[68]

St. Thomas Aquinas (1226-1274) addresses the problem in much the same fashion as his contemporary, Bonaventure. First he indicates that a perpetual (natural) impediment must be absolute.[69] But then he admits *maleficium* is relative because it does not depend on a necessary cause.[70] Yet, such a *maleficium* could still be perpetual and would form part of the impediment of impotence.[71] Such a line of reasoning implicitly contains a shift in the notion of impediment from something that necessarily physically prevents marriage to impediment as a reason, a principle, an entity of the juridic order.

St. Raymond of Pennafort († 1275) also shows that he understands the impediment of impotence in more than a physiological sense: he takes pains to point out that "impossibilitas coëundi" can be a "vitium animi" as well as "corporis."

---

non est a prima complexione. *Sed frigiditas quae est ex complexione et naturaliter inest ... haec est quae impedit, et haec est inseparabilis et perpetua."* (Emphasis mine).

[66] *Ibid.*, q. 2, resp., pp. 759-760: « Dupliciter autem fit maleficium perpetuum: aut respectu omnis mulieris, et sic reddit inhabilem ad omnem; aut respectu uxoris, et *sic reddit inhabilem ad illam, sed non ad omnes ...*" (Emphasis mine); *ibid.*, ad 4um, p. 760: "Ad illud quod ultimo obicitur, quod aequaliter se habet vis illa ad omnes, dicendum breviter quod verum est; et *si impediretur naturali impedimento, aequaliter impediretur ad omnes; sed* quia daemoniaco impeditur ... cum sortiaria respectu personae determinatae facit sortilegium, diabolus in actu illo praesto est et non in aliis ..."* (Emphasis mine).

[67] *Ibid.*, resp., p. 760: "Concedendae igitur sunt rationes ostendentes quod maleficium praestat impedimentum matrimonio."

[68] *Ibid.*, art. 2, q. 2, p. 758: "Item *ubicumque talis causa, ibi talis effectus; sed frigiditas* vel arctitudo *impediebat et dirimebat* propter impotentiam reddendi debitum; ergo, *cum talis causa sit in maleficiatis,* videtur etc."* (Emphasis mine).

[69] THOMAS AQUINAS, *Supplementum Tertiae Partis Summae Theologicae*, q. 58 art. 1, ad 5: "... non potest esse perpetuum impedimentum naturale viro respectu unius personae et non respectu alterius."

[70] *Ibid.*, art. 2, ad 4um: "... maleficum quandoque potest praestare ad omnes impedimentum, *quandoque ad unam tantum: quia diabolus voluntaria causa est, non ex necessitate naturae agens."* (Emphasis mine).

[71] *Ibid.*, resp.

Moreover, "impossibilitas coëundi" is an impediment precisely because it prevents the ends of marriage from being attained.[72] *Maleficium* can be perpetual, and is a form of this "impossibilitas coëundi" because it prevents the accomplishment of the ends of marriage in the same way as the other forms of the impediment.[73]

Throughout the period 1200-1600, the controversy whether *maleficium* was perpetual, whether *maleficium* was a form of the impediment of impotence continued. The realization gradually deepened, first among the theologians, then among the canonists, that *maleficium* was truly a form of the impediment. By the early part of the seventeenth century, general agreement was finally reached, that *maleficium*, a relative and biologically undetermined form of impotence, truly constituted the impediment as well as such natural conditions as *frigiditas* and *arctatio*.[74]

### C. CONCLUSION: THE PERPETUITY OF THE IMPEDIMENT OF IMPOTENCE MUST BE UNDERSTOOD AS A TRUE JURIDIC CONCEPT RATHER THAN A SITUATION OF FACT

**1.** *The Notion of the Impediment of Impotence, Itself, Is Recognized as Something More than the Physical Inability to Have Sexual Relations*

The review of the literature on impotence shows that during the period from 1200-1600 there was a gradual, almost imperceptible change in the understanding of the meaning of the term "impediment of impotence."

---

[72] RAYMOND of PENNAFORT, *Summa*, lib. IV, tit. 16, p. 513: "Quum enim omne matrimonium, aut causa suscipiendae prolis, aut causa incontinentiae fiat, impossibilitas coëundi utramque causam removet...."

[73] *Ibid.*, p. 515, n. 2.

[74] *Maleficium* was classified as a relative form of impotence based on an accidental rather than necessary cause. Cf. foonote 52 of this chapter. The following authors accept accidental, relative impotence as a form of the impediment of impotence: Hostiensis, Bonaventure, Thomas Aquinas, Raymond of Pennafort, Panormitanus, Soto, Henriquez, Sanchez, Pontius, Castro Palao, Laymann, Barbosa, Perez ab Unanoa, Reiffenstuel, Salmanticenses, Schmier, Pirhing, Schmalzgrueber, and Alphonsus de Liguori. Thus the acceptance of relative impotence as nullifying can be considered common doctrine. For exact reference, see sections of the text dealing with each author's treatment of *maleficium*.

At first the *impediment* was identified with the *condition*. The impediment was equated with its cause; accordingly, "the impediment" meant a physical condition which absolutely prevented sexual intercourse with anyone at all, at any time whatsoever.

By the first half of the seventeenth century, the term "impediment" could no longer be identified with this exclusively concrete physical meaning. Both the *praxis Ecclesiae* as well as doctrinal consensus among the authors had by now led to the full recognition of relative impotence as constituting the "impediment." The acceptance of natural relative impotence (*arctatio*), while still preserving the physiological basis of the former notion of impediment, showed that such a form of impotence qualified as "impediment" because it prevented the ends of marriage from being attained by this particular couple. An "impediment" is something which prevents *this* marriage, even if it should not prevent *every* marriage.

The acceptance of accidental, i.e. not natural, not biologically determined, relative impotence (*maleficium*) as constituting the "impediment," completely liberated this term from identification with the concrete physical condition which was the cause of the impossibility of sexual relations. This showed that the essential factor in "impediment" was the impossibility of sexual intercourse itself, rather than its cause. Now "impediment" could be understood in its real dimension, as something which prevented the ends of marriage from being attained. Finally, it became possible to recognize that the "impediment" of impotence is the *moral* (rather than physical) inability to assume rights and obligations to place acts *per se aptos ad prolis generationem*.

## 2. *The Juridic Meaning of Perpetual*

The object of this chapter is to understand as best we can the meaning of Innocent III's phrase: "impedimentum perpetuum." Perpetual used here is an adjective, and it will always signify a mode, a way of being of the "impediment". The ordinary and principal connotation of perpetual is: to endure in space and time. Thus perpetual impediment would be one that endures in time. Yet the literature of this period shows that the authors used the term "perpetual" principally to connote an impediment that was natural, biologically determined, congenital.    When they spoke of perpetual impediment, they meant primarily to indicate a condition which *necessarily* prevented intercourse; of course, in the nature of things such a condition would also generally be stable, enduring and antecedent, because congenital.

When the term "impediment" came to be understood in an abstract, conceptual sense as a relationship to the ends of marriage, "perpetual," too, acquired a new meaning.    In this new conception, "perpetual" would no longer indicate the natural stability in time of a condition which necessarily prevents the marital act; rather, "perpetual" would now indicate a concept qualifying or modifying the relationship of a particular situation of impotence to the ends of marriage.    The concept of the perpetuity of impotence, then, is the definition and delimitation of the principal circumstances in which a particular case of impotence is seen to be incompatible with the ends of marriage.    Perpetuity is a quality of a particular situation of impotence which specifies and determines precisely why there is a moral inability to assume the rights and obligations to place acts *per se aptos ad prolis generationem.*

"Antecedent" is no longer automatically implied by "perpetual," because "perpetual" no longer connotes a natural congenital cause.    Hence antecedence must be distinguished from perpetuity and recognized in its own right as a *requirement* of the impediment of impotence.    Both qualities are necessary to specify and determine *all* the circumstances in which a particular case of impotence is incompatible with the ends of marriage.

The perpetuity of the impediment of impotence can, therefore, be defined as a true juridic concept specifying the circumstances in which the moral inability to assume rights and obligations to place *actos per se aptos ad prolis generationem* is truly present.

CHAPTER THREE

DESCRIPTIVE DEFINITION OF PERPETUITY AND ITS
IDENTIFICATION WITH THE CONCEPT OF
EXTRAORDINARY MEANS

After the year 1600, canonical literature reflects a new type
of response to the question posed to Innocent III in the case
of the *mulier arcta*. The thought patterns and methods of
argumentation used show beyond doubt that perpetuity was
seen, at least from this time on, as a concept and not as a mere
physical fact.[1] This is by no means to assert that all of these
authors fully recognized and appreciated this. The connatural
tendency to equate the impediment with its physical cause
bolstered by the authority of concrete decisions of decretal law
and the almost universal teaching of previous centuries would
make even the boldest thinker hesitate to unequivocally assert
that perpetuity was a juridic concept. Even today, many would
still understand perpetuity in an exclusively time related sense.

Nonetheless, the authors in the early 1600's begin to treat
Innocent III's phrase "...impedimentum illud non erat perpetuum..." in a new way, according to the second interpretation
we have seen above, i.e. as a definition. By their explanations

---

[1] The following authors by their clear and unequivocal statements
that the impediment can still be perpetual, even though potency should
actually be regained, show beyond doubt that they considered perpe-
tuity to be a concept not a mere physical fact. Cf. AEGIDIUS DE CONINCK,
*De sacramentis et censuris*, II (Lugduni, 1619), disp. 31, dub. 7, p. 813, n. 85;
FERDINAND CASTRO PALAO, *Opus morale, de virtutibus et vitiis contrariis*,
Pars 5ª (Lugduni, ²1649), tract. 28, disp. 4, punct. 14, p. 162, n. 4; MARTI-
NUS PEREZ ab UNANOA, *Opus morale theologicum de sancto matrimonii
sacramento* (Lugduni, 1646), disp 37, sect. 1, p. 409, n. 3; LAYMANN,
*Theologia moralis*, (Venetiis, 1719), lib. 5, tract 10, pars 4, cap. 11, p.
383, n. 1; ANACLETUS REIFFENSTUEL, *Ius canonicum universum*, IV (Antwerpiae, ²1755), lib. IV, tit. 15, p. 114, n. 5; SCHMALZGRUEBER, *Ius ecclesiasticum universum*, IX, tom. 4, pars 3, tit. 15, p. 173, n. 44; ALPHONSUS
DE LIGUORI, *Theologia moralis*, ed. Leonard Gaudé, IV (Romae, ²1912),
lib. 6, tract. 6, cap. 3, dub. 2, p. 226, n. 1096.

5

of Innocent's phrase they were in reality giving us a descriptive definition of the content of the concept of perpetuity. In other sections of their works, these same authors speak of the notion of ordinary and extraordinary means; some even use these terms in their treatment of perpetuity. Our object in this chapter is to investigate the definition given by these authors and see what relationship there is between perpetuity and the notion of extraordinary means.

### A. DEFINITION OF PERPETUITY DRAWN FROM THEOLOGICAL AND CANONICAL LITERATURE, ESPECIALLY FROM 1600-1900

Read as a definition, and with the negatives transposed for the sake of clarity, Innocent III's comment on perpetuity is understood as follows:

> A perpetual impediment is one that cannot be removed by natural human means without bodily danger.

The definition thus has two principal connotations. First, the impediment is perpetual, if, *in fact*, no remedy exists for it; thus, as long as the physical condition of impotency actually endures until death, the impediment will have been perpetual. This is the most direct and literal understanding of the text. It is also the physiological interpretation that we discussed earlier. Such an interpretation is recognized as valid by all, for it describes one of the conditions, one of the circumstances which the concept of perpetuity comprises. Thus in order to explain why the first marriage of the *mulier arcta* must be re-established if potency is regained in the second marriage, most authors use Innocent III's own reasoning: the first marriage was valid and must be re-established because experience has shown that the impotent condition, and hence the impediment, was not actually perpetual, i.e. permanently enduring until the death of the person declared impotent.[2]

---

[2] Cf. HOSTIENSIS, *Summa aurea*, lib. IV, tit. *de frigidis*, p. 317, n. 16; RICARDUS de MEDIAVILLA, *Super quatuor libros Sententiarum*, IV, dist. 34, art. 2, q. 1, p. 476; DURANDUS a SANCTO PORCIANO, *Petri Lombardi Sententias theologicas commentariorum libri IV*, dist. 34, q. 2, p. 380, n. 6; MARTINUS BONACINA, *Opera omnia*, I: *Tractatus de magno matrimonii sacramento* (Venetiis, 1728), q. 3, punct. 13, p. 298, n. 8; CONSTANTINUS

The second connotation seems at first to be absolutely contradictory to the first which we have just explained; it reads: the impediment is perpetual, even though a remedy for the impotent condition *does* exist. The addition of a modifying or qualifying clause takes away this apparent contradiction. Thus we may read the definition according to this connotation as follows:

> An impediment will also be perpetual, even though a remedy for the impotent condition exists, provided that this remedy is so extraordinary, so rare, that it would be physically and/or morally impossible for the average man to be able to use it.

In this sentence we have a descriptive definition of perpetuity. The concept of perpetuity is here presented in a nutshell. Our aim in this section will be to investigate the teaching of the authors on the elements of this definition as they were historically expressed. This historical expression consisted of three conditions or circumstances expressed in the modifying clause of Innocent: "praeter divinum miraculum, per opus humanum, absque corporali periculo." We will now investigate the meaning of each of these.

1. *The Impediment of Impotence Is Perpetual If the Only Remedy for the Impotent Condition Is Something Beyond Human Powers*

It seems quite evident to us that the phrase "praeter divinum miraculum" modifies Innocent's sentence to read: the impediment is perpetual if the impotent condition is cured by a miracle. Yet in the context of the age in which perpetual impediment meant a defect that was naturally permanent, incurable, it is not surprising to note that very few commentators adopt a reading which would in effect call a condition perpetual even after it no longer really existed, because it had been cured by a miracle. The *Glossa ordinaria in Decretales*, Innocent IV and Hostiensis all repeat the text without commenting on the effect a miracle would have on the perpetuity of the impediment. Thomas Aquinas seems to be one of the first to point out different consequences for the perpetuity of the im-

---

RONCAGLIA, *Universa moralis theologia* (Lucae, 1730), tom. 2, tract 21, q. 4, c. 6, p. 203.

pediment if a divine rather than human means should have
been used to remove the impotent condition.[3]

Antonius a Butrio (1338-1408) seems to be the first who
explicitly concentrated on reading Innocent's phrase with the
reverse emphasis characteristic of the second connotation:

> Nota septimo, quod illud non dicitur perpetuum impedimen-
> tum quod praeter divinum miraculum absque periculo corporis
> reparatur.  Et sic *econverso* nota *quod illud dicitur perpetuum*
> impedimentum, *quod per divinum tantum miraculum est repa-
> rabile*, sed forte est reparabile, sed non sine mortis periculo.
> *Et sic illud dicitur non possible, quod dependet a solo Dei
> miraculo.* [4]

Yet he still did not have the courage to explicitly state the
logical consequence of this: the impediment is perpetual, even
if the impotent condition is actually cured by a miracle, because such a cure must be considered ordinarily impossible and
the condition, therefore, ordinarily perpetual.

Thomas Sanchez (1551-1610) is one of the principal authors
on the subject of the sacrament of Matrimony; it was he who
gave the first clear exposition why relative impotence was sufficient to constitute a matrimonial impediment.[5]  So, too, he
was the first to clearly and explicitly state that the physical
fact of restored potency was no hindrance to recognition of the
existence of the impediment: the marriage was still invalid, the
impediment perpetual, even though potency had been actually
restored, because the restoration came about as a result of a
miracle.[6]

---

[3] THOMAS AQUINAS, *Commentarius posterior super libros Sententiarum Petri Lombardi*, dist. 34, q. 1, art. 2, ad 3um: « Ad tertium, dicendum quod maleficium reputatur impedimentum perpetuum, quando
*opere humano* non potest remedium adhiberi, licet possit *opere divino.*"
(Emphasis mine); cf. also IOANNIS ANDREAE, *In IV decretalium librum
novella commentaria,* IV, lib. IV, tit. 15, c. 7, p. 51, n. 16.

[4] ANTONIUS a BUTRIO, *In libros decretalium commentarii,* VI, lib. IV,
tit. 15, c. 6, p. 41, n. 9. (Emphasis mine).

[5] SANCHEZ, *Disputationum de santo matrimonii sacramento,* II, lib.
7, disp. 93, p. 339, n. 3.

[6] *Ibid.,* p. 341, n. 8: "Hinc deducitur, matrimonium initum cum ita
impotenti viro, aut cum muliere sic arcta, ut illi defectui absque miraculo subveniri non possit esse tamquam irritum dissolvendum, *etsi ante
dissolutionem cessarit iam per miraculum impotentia illa".* (Emphasis
mine); Also, DE CONINCK, *De sacramentis et censuris,* II, disp. 31, dub.
7, p. 813, n. 85; RONCAGLIA, *Universa moralis theologia,* tom. 2, tract. 21,
q. 4, c. 6, p. 202.

Dominicus Soto (1494-1560) had really said the same thing earlier, but in an oblique way. He also provided a reason why the impediment should still be considered perpetual, even though the impotent condition had been cured by a miracle: the impediment must still be perpetual, because the nature or essence of marriage (its validity or invalidity) cannot depend on a fortuitous event such as a miracle.[7]

Ferdinand Castro Palao (1581-1633) also explicitly states that impotency cured by miracle still qualifies as a perpetual impediment. Once again he repeats the reason given by Soto and Sanchez: the impediment is perpetual because one cannot be expected to wait for a miracle since this is something beyond the nature of things.[8]

Paulus Laymann (1574-1635), too, teaches that the impediment is perpetual because a cure dependent on a miracle is something that is morally speaking impossible, and therefore should be regarded as non-existent.[9]

Thus it is the clear and evident teaching of these canonists and theologians that, at least in this instance, it is not the presence or absence of the physical condition of impotence, but rather the concept which is determinative of the perpetuity of the impediment.

There has been no significant change in this position from that time to the present. It is interesting to note, however, that there is considerably less discussion of the possibility of a miraculous cure during the late 1700's. Perhaps we can ascribe this to the mood of the times known as the Enlightenment. At any rate, Franciscus Schmier (1680-1728), a Benedictine professor in Salzburg, makes no mention of a miracle or the possibility of a miraculous cure for impotence in his work,

---

[7] Soto, *In Quartum Sententiarum*, II, dist. 34, q. 1, art. 2, p. 245, n. 4.

[8] "...quia miraculum cum sit praeter rerum naturam expectari nequit necdum comprobari...." Castro Palao, *Opus morale, de virtutibus et vitiis contrariis*, tract. 28, disp. 4, punc. 14, p. 161, n. 2.

[9] Laymann, *Theologia moralis*, lib. 5, tr. 10, pars 4, cap. 11, p. 383, n. 1: "...quod dixi impotentia perpetua, qualis est quae neque arte medica, neque consuetis Ecclesiae exorcismos tolli potest, etsi tolli possit cum periculo vitae, aut gravissimi morbi, impossibilis censetur curatio; similiter si per illicitam incantationem, quia, quod iure non possumus, id absolute non posse censemus. *Denique etsi per miraculum tolli possit*, nihilominus, moraliter rem aestimando impossibilis est curatio." (Emphasis mine)

*Iurisprudentia canonico-civilis.*[10] Honoratus Tournely (1658-1729)
in his definition of perpetual impotence does not mention a
miraculous means as a possible remedy for this condition;
later on, however, he does admit, by way of exception, that if
a person involved in a second marriage had been cured by a
miracle, then the first marriage would not have to be re-
established.[11] Undoubtedly this low key treatment of the miraculous was due to a desire to show more faith in the natural
sciences and a lesser readiness to attribute cures to supernatural
intervention.

### 2. *The Impediment of Impotence Is Perpetual, If the Only Remedy for the Impotent Condition Is Something Sinful or Illicit*

The second qualifying phrase used by Innocent III was
"per opus humanum." This immediately reinforces the idea
that the impotent condition must be impossible to remove by
ordinary, natural, rather than supernatural means, in order to
qualify as a perpetual impediment. Comments about the meaning of this phrase were rather rare before the time of Soto.
Quite probably, one reason for this was the method of commentary used by the early canonists; they did not systematically
discuss all elements of a problem, rather they concentrated
on textual exegesis and particular aspects concerning the case
in question.

Thus, once again, it was the case of the *mulier arcta* which
was the starting point for later clarification of how illicit means
of removal of the condition of impotence would affect the perpetuity of the impediment. Innocent III provides a basis for
further speculation on the question: Is the impediment still
perpetual, if it can only be removed by a sinful means? He
ponders whether the first husband of the *mulier arcta* would
be justified in refusing to accept her back because her second
marriage could be considered adultery. He concludes that

---

[10] Franciscus Schmier, *Iurisprudentia canonico-civilis seu ius canonicum universum*, III (Salisburgi, ²1729), lib. 4, tract 3, cap. 2, sect. 2,
pp. 106-113.

[11] Honoratus Tournely, *De universa theologia morali*, II (Venetiis,
1746), cap. 14, compare p. 746 with p. 750. For a similar treatment of
the material, see Lucius Ferraris, *Prompta bibilotheca canonica, juridica, moralis, theologica etc.* (Romae, ²1788) s. v. *Matrimonium*, art. VI,
p. 205, n. 52.

such a charge would be highly debatable; adultery cannot be presumed in such circumstances.[12] The only criterion that he wishes to take into account is the fact that she has had sexual intercourse; she is therefore potent; she must be returned to the first husband.

The *Glossa on the Decretals* also uses the one standard of regained potency as the basis of decision about the perpetuity of the impediment and the validity of the first marriage. No consideration about the morality or immorality of the means used to render her potent is allowed to influence the decision. The Glossators propose a new problem: suppose she and her first husband were still unable to have relations after she had been restored to him? They resolve the problem with a suggestion that seems quite immoral, though perhaps technically legal: she should live with the first husband for another three-year test period; if they still were unable to have relations she could separate from him, but if she were ever able to have sexual relations again with anyone at any time, she must immediately again be restored to the first husband. They explicitly state that this procedure could go on an infinite number of times.[13]

Innocent IV was likewise only concerned with the fact of potency. If the woman were found capable of sexual intercourse she must be returned to her first husband.[14]

From this review of the early commentators it appears that the morality or immorality of the means used to regain potency was not considered to have any bearing on the perpetuity of

---

[12] X, IV, 15, c. 6: "Nam si tantum simplici verbo se promisit continentiam servaturam, et postea in conspectu Ecclesiae nupsit memorato G., quamdiu articulus iste dubitabilis erat, *praesumi non debet, quod fornicaretur cum illo,* sed amodo non debet cum illo aliquatenus remanere." (Emphasis mine)

[13] *Glossa in Decretales* in X, IV, 15, c. 6 s. v. *fornicario modo.* In discussing this problem, Hostiensis records an opinion that she need only be restored to the first husband twice because he would have no further recourse after two conforming sentences; he does not seem to agree and adds simply: "...elapso triennio restitueretur secundo sine spe restitutionis primo faciendae...." See *Summa aurea,* lib. IV, tit. *de frigidis,* p. 317, n. 13; also IOANNIS ANDREAE, *In IV decretalium librum novella commentaria,* IV, lib. IV, tit. 15, c. 6, p. 51 n. 26.

[14] "...melius placet, quod... sive per concubitum alterius viri ...reddatur apta, *primo semper restituenda est...."* INNOCENT IV, *Commentaria in V libros decretalium,* lib. IV, tit. 15, c. 6, p. 569, n. 1. (Emphasis mine).

the impediment. For them the fact of subsequent sexual intercourse was sufficient to destroy the perpetuity of the impediment.

Later jurists began to pose this question of the effect on
perpetuity of the morality or immorality of the means used to
restore potency in a different context. During the controversy
about the perpetuity of *maleficium* the question was raised:
Can we not consider a *maleficium* perpetual, even though it was
actually removed, if the removal came about by such a sinful
and illicit means as making use of another witch's spell? Both
Thomas Aquinas and Bonaventure solve this question by using
a moral principle as a guide: it would be immoral to invoke
the aid of the devil either directly or through a witch; therefore the *maleficium* must be considered irremovable, perpetual.[15]

Soto seems to be the first author who broadened the above
principle by applying it to *all* the means of removal of the
impediment: he states that even though the impotency should
be removed by an act of fornication, or by a magic spell,
the impediment would still be perpetual: "... quia impedimentum quod non nisi per peccatum potest tolli, non censetur aufe-
ribile." [16]

Sanchez, too, sees this principle as a general one applying
to all methods of removal of the impediment: the impediment
will still be perpetual, even if it is removed by a sinful or illicit
human action. To explain why, he quotes the axiom which will
be repeated by a whole series of authors who concur in this
interpretation of "per opus humanum": "... id solum dicamur
posse, quod licite possumus praestare...." [17]

---

[15] "Et tamen, si posset per maleficium remedium adhiberi, *nihilominus perpetuum reputaretur*: quia nullo modo debet aliquis daemonis
auxilium per maleficium invocare." Thomas Aquinas, *Supplementum
Tertiae Partis Summae Theologicae*, q. 58, art. 2, ad 3um (emphasis
mine); BONAVENTURA, *Liber IV Sententiarum*, dist. 34, art. 2, q. 2, ad
2um: "...diabolus ad hoc non debet invocari nec eius patrocinium im-
plorari, *hinc* est *quod tale maleficium dicitur esse perpetuum.*" (Emphasis mine)

[16] SOTO, *In Quartum Sententiarum*, II, dist. 34, q. 1, art. 2, p. 245.

[17] SANCHEZ, *Disputationum de sancto matrimonii sacramento*, II, lib.
7, disp. 93, p. 341, n. 9: "Secundo deducitur censeri impedimentum perpetuum ac proinde dirimi coniugium ratione illius, quando nequit auferri per opus humanum absque peccato. Cum enim id solum dicamur
posse, quod licite possumus praestare; *impedimentum quod sine peccato auferri minime valet, dicitur impossibile ablatu ac perpetuum.*"
(Emphasis mine); Authors who cite this axiom are: BONACINA, *Tracta-

The later writers, probably realizing that such an interpretation is almost self-evident, simply limit themselves to declaring that the impediment is perpetual if removed by an illicit means.[18]

Thus, once again, it is the clear and evident teaching of the canonists and theologians that the presence or absence of the physical condition of impotence is not the determining factor in deciding whether an impediment is perpetual or not; the decisive factor is the concept of perpetuity, which in this case gives no juridic value to an illegal or illegitimate act.

3. *The Impediment of Impotence Is Perpetual If the Only Remedy for the Impotent Condition Is One that Is Dangerous, One that Would Involve Bodily Risk*

In this section we will deal with the historical interpretation given to the third phrase of Innocent III's definition of perpetuity: "absque corporali periculo." The meaning of this phrase is very complex because it really involves two questions: 1) Do the authors agree that removal of the physical condition of impotence by a dangerous means still leaves the impediment perpetual? 2) How great a danger must be involved before a means is considered dangerous enough to qualify as a condition affecting the perpetuity of the impediment? Then there are

---

*tus de magno matrimonii sacramento,* q. 3, pt. 13, p. 297, n. 2; CASTRO PALAO, *Opus morale, de virtutibus et virtiis contrariis,* Pars 5ª, tract. 28, disp. 4, punc. 14, p. 161, n. 2: "... quia id possumus, quod iure possumus. Cum autem peccatum iure non facere possumus, *nequaquam est possibile illus impedimentum removere.*" (Emphasis mine); LAYMANN, *Theologia moralis,* lib. 5, tr. 10, pars 4, c. 11, p. 383, n. 1; PEREZ ab UNANOA, *Opus morale theologicum de sancto matrimoni sacramento,* disp. 37, sect. 1, p. 409, n. 3; REIFFENSTUEL, *Ius canonicum universum,* IV, lib. 4, tit. 15, p. 114, n. 5; SALMANTICENSES, *Cursus theologiae moralis,* II, tr. 9, c. 12, punc. 10, p. 161, n. 115: "... quia *quod sine peccato fieri nequit, absolute impossibile* reputatur: quia id possumus quod licite possumus." (Emphasis mine); Cf. also BASILIUS PONTIUS, *De sacramento matrimonii tractatus* (Lugduni, 1640), lib. 7, cap. 61, p. 442, n. 3: "... tunc perpetuus iudicari debet, quando medio aliquo facili, et licito secundum iura, talique ut prudentia et aequitas admittendum iubeat, tolli non potest."

[18] Cf. SCHMIER, *Iurisprudentia canonico-civilis seu ius canonicum universum,* III, lib. 4, tract. 3, cap. 2, sect, 2, p. 107, n. 80; FERRARIS, *Promta biblioteca* s. v. *Matrimonium,* art. VI, p. 203; MICHAEL ROSSET, *De sacramento matrimonii, tractatus dogmaticus, moralis, canonicus, liturgicus et iudiciarius,* II (Parisiis, 1895), p. 558, n. 1379.

corollary questions: Must it be a danger to life? Or to health? Does either of the parties have an obligation to submit to a dangerous means of removing the condition?

### a) *The Presence of Danger Suffices to Declare the Impediment Perpetual*

Our first question would seem to have a simple straight forward response: everyone must agree that a remedy involving danger leaves the impediment perpetual because this is explicitly stated in Innocent III's text.

The historical answer was not quite that simple because several dangerous situations were envisioned and the solutions varied accordingly.

In the case of *arctatio*, i.e. severe disproportion of the genital organs of husband and wife, a danger could arise from too arduous attempts on the part of the husband to consummate the marriage. There is almost universal consent on the part of the authors that the danger arising from such a situation would leave the impediment perpetual. Even one of the staunchest advocates of the biological, temporal understanding of perpetuity, Innocent IV, grudgingly admits that, if in a very rare case a marriage could only be consummated by such efforts as would endanger the bride's life, he would consider such an impediment perpetual.[19] He admits this only grudgingly because he is still preoccupied with the fact that the first marriage must be re-established if the woman ever does succeed in having sexual relations with anyone. In short, he says it would be better not to bother asking about such things as the danger involved, or the relative disproportion of genital organs; all one should do is determine whether the woman was truly *arctam*, that is, so defective that sexual intercourse would be completely impossible for her with anyone at any time. Thus one would have a clear principle for solving like cases: if the woman were ever found capable of subsequent sexual relations, the first marriage must be re-established.[20]

---

[19] INNOCENT IV, *Commentaria in V libros decretalium*, lib. IV, tit. 15, c. 6, p. 570, n. 1. Cf. also HOSTIENSIS, *Summa aurea*, lib. IV, tit. *de frigidis*, p. 315, n. 3; RAYMOND of PENNAFORT, *Summa*, lib. IV, tit. 16, p. 514; PANORMITANUS, *Commentaria in libros decretalium*, VII, lib. IV, rubrica *de frigidis*, c. 6, p. 61, n. 19.

[20] INNOCENT IV, *Commentaria in V libros decretalium*, lib. IV, tit. 15, c. 6, p. 571, n. 7: "...per sententiam quam tulimus in hoc negotio, in

A second situation envisioned by the authors involving danger would be one in which the physical condition, usually *arctatio* consisting of an impenetrable hymen, could be remedied only by perilous medicines or methods, such as surgery. Here again the early commentators set down a quite simple principle: the impediment was not perpetual if the woman had, in fact, been helped by the medicines or cured by the operation, notwithstanding the danger involved.[21]

Once again it is Soto and Sanchez who first explicitly state that the presence or absence of the physical condition of impotence is not determinative of the perpetuity of the impediment.[22] Rather it is the reality of the presence or absence of danger as determined by competent medical experts which specifies and determines whether or not this situation constitutes a true impediment, a true incompatibility with the ends of marriage.[23]

---

qua non discussimus de corporali periculo, neque de simili viro, sed tantum quia nobis constituit mulierem non arctam esse, primo eam sibi restituendam decrevimus." Also, *ibid.*, p. 569, n. 1.

[21] *Ibid.*: "...plus placet quod idonea sit quia perpetuum impedimentum non habet, unde dicimus quod separata a viro propter arctationem si incidatur etiam cum periculo, tamen priori viro restituenda est...." IOANNIS ANDREAE, *In IV decretalium librum novella commentaria*, IV, lib. IV, tit. 15, c. 6, p. 51, n. 29.

[22] SOTO, *In Quartum Sententiarum*, II, dict. 34, q. 1, art. 2, p. 246, seen in relationship to p. 245; SANCHEZ, *Disputationum de sancto matrimonii sacramento*, II, lib. 7, disp. 93, p. 341, n. 15: "Quarto deducitur, si iudicio medicorum impedimentum impotentiae medicabile sit absque corporali periculo, quamvis femina renuat incisionem aut medicamenta necessaria, quibus apta reddatur viro, firmum esse matrimonium. *Quod eius firmitas ac valor minime ex feminae voluntate pendeant: sed ex ipsa rei natura, iuxta quam impedimentum illud temporale est, utpote quod potest per artem absque corporali periculo tolli*". (Emphasis mine); Cf. also, LAYMANN, *Theologia moralis*, lib. 5, tr. 10, pars 4, c. 11, p. 383 n. 1.

[23] BONACINA, *Tractatus de magno matrimonii sacramento*, q. 3, punct. 13, p. 297, n. 5: "...nam attendenda est rei natura, secundum quam in praesenti casu impedimentum non est perpetuum, sed temporale, cum possit arte humana auferri absque probabili vitae periculo."; CASTRO PALAO, *Opus morale, de virtutibus et vitiis contrariis*, tract. 28, disp. 4, punct. 14, p. 162, n. 5: "...quia impedimenti perpetuitas non pendet ex voluntate patientis impedimentum, *neque ex eo quod tollatur, vel non tollatur, sed ex eo quod spectata rei natura tolli, vel non tolli possit absque vitae periculo*." (Emphasis mine); SALMANTICENSES, *Cursus theologiae moralis*, II, tr. 9, c. 12, punc. 10, p. 161, n. 115: "...quia perpetuitas impotentiae dirimens, non ex voluntate, sed ex natura rei dependet, neque attenditur, quod tollatur, vel non, sed quod tolli possit..."

Later authors could then articulate the reasons why real danger would constitute a true impediment: 1) because it would be something morally impossible, something equivalent to an immoral act, to expect a person to fulfill the ends of marriage if the only possible way to do this were by exposing himself to danger;[24] 2) because no one could be presumed to have obliged himself to fulfilling the ends of marriage if the only possible way to do this were by exposing himself to danger.[25]

A few authors also discuss other situations involving danger which in their view might qualify to constitute a perpetual impediment. They ask for example: Does danger to the life of the woman due to the inability to bear the rigors of the

---

[24] PONTIUS, *De sacramento matrimonii tractatus*, lib. 7, c. 61, p. 442, n. 3: "Quod enim fieri non potest, nisi aliquo praeternaturali medio illicito, aut cum vitae periculo, aut cum gravi aliquo inconvenienti, id nec ius nec prudentia, nec ratio fieri posse dictat, sed respuit, nec executioni mandandum censet. Unde sicut lethale aliquod vulnus medico incurabili est, quamvis chirurgo forte non sit, et e contra gravis aliquis morbus extra remedium erit chirurgo, quamvis non censeatur a medico: ita merito adynaton est iuri et aequitati, quod secundum leges illius fieri non potest, id enim possumus, quod iure possumus."

[25] REIFFENSTUEL, *Ius canonicum universum*, IV, lib. IV, tit. 15, p. 120, n. 67: "...quia nulla pars coniugum videtur se obligare ad copulam cum tanta sanitatis iactura..."; ALPHONSUS DE LIGUORI, *Theologia moralis*, lib. 6, tract. 6, cap. 3, dub. 2, p. 227, n. 1097: "Ratio, quia impotentia eo casu non est a voluntate, sed ab ipsa natura: ex contractu enim matrimonii, videtur mulier non ad plus se obligasse quam ad reddendum debitum per media ordinaria. Unde, quando non potest fieri apta nisi per medium extraordinariam et periculosam gravis morbi, tunc censetur illa ex ipsa natura impotens ad matrimonium."; RONCAGLIA, *Universa moralis theologia*, tom. 2, tract. 21, q. 4, c. 6, p. 203: "Sed puto neque teneri pati cum gravissimae infirmitatis periculo, cum credi non possit voluisse se ad hoc obligare."; Tournely sums up both of these reasons in explaining why a woman would not be required to submit to a dangerous operation in order to remove an otherwise perpetual physical condition. Cf. *De universa theologia morali*, II (Venetiis, 1746), c. 14, p. 750: "...quia ut impedimentum reputetur temporale, requiri videtur, ut non solum sine vitae periculo, sed etiam illaesis honestatis et pudicitiae legibus auferri possit: atqui: cum ad auferendum impedimentum praerequiritur incisio, medium, quod non nisi violatis honestatis et verecundiae legibus adhiberi potest. Quid enim turpius, quam ut virgo nuda oculis et manibus chirurgi subiciatur, et incisionem foedam simul ac gravem pati cogatur. Certe paucae sunt sexus personae, quae hac conditione, si ante matrimonium sibi subeunda proponeretur, contrahere vellent." Cf. also HENRIQUEZ, *Summae theologiae moralis*, I, lib. 12, c. 7, p. 725, n. 8, nota k: "...quia foemina non intendit cum certo vitae periculo transferre corpus in virum, neque id licere."

later stages of pregnancy and birth constitute a perpetual impediment of impotence because of the danger involved? Or would danger to offspring, for example, arising from the inability to successfully bring pregnancy to term? These problems do not technically concern impotence as we have defined it: the inability to engage in sexual intercourse. Consequently we remit the reader to the appropriate sources.[26]

### b) *Only Serious Danger of Death or Grave Illness Suffices to Constitute a Perpetual Impediment*

As a logical consequence of the admission that the impediment would be perpetual if it could be removed only by a dangerous means, the practical problem of deciding the amount of danger involved immediately arose. Hence most authors soon saw the need to determine how much danger was meant by the phrase "corporali periculo."

Innocent III seems to indicate in the very text under consideration that the danger must be: "... non solummodo levis, sed forte tam gravis, ut ex ea mortis periculum timeatur." [27]

The *Glossa ordinaria on the Decretals* and all later commentaries universally admit that it must be a serious, grave danger.[28]

Innocent IV, however, gives a very strict interpretation of grave danger — so strict that for him it means death itself. In explaining how he would understand the danger of an operation to affect the perpetuity of the impediment, he says that the impediment would only have been perpetual if the woman had, in fact, *died* as a result of the attempt to cure it. If she lived through the danger and the operation, then, of course, the impediment would only have been temporary because she

---

[26] *Ibid.*; SANCHEZ, *Disputationum de sancto matrimonii sacramento*, II, lib. 7, disp. 92, p. 338, n. 27, and p. 339, n. 28-29; DE CONINCK, *De sacramentis et censuris*, II, disp. 31, dub. 7, p. 813, n. 86; CASTRO PALAO, *Opus morale, de virtutibus et vitiis contrariis*, Pars 5ª, tract. 28, disp. 4, punct. 14, p. 162, n. 13.

[27] IV, 15, c. 6.

[28] *Glossa ordinaria in Decretales* in X, IV, 15, c. 6 s. v. *corporali periculo:* "Ubi vero grave periculum timeretur non est matrimonium: sed ubi levi periculo potest removeri, debet illud pati." See also, ANTONIUS a BUTRIO, *In libros decretalium commentarii*, lib. IV, tit. 15, c. 6, p. 41, n. 22. From their general treatment all the other authors dealt with show that they understand that the danger must be a grave danger.

is, in fact, alive and well and the condition of impotence has been cured.[29]

Once more it is Soto who leads the way to a change in viewpoint. He states that the danger must be a real danger, but it need not be exclusively a danger of death; the danger of a very serious illness such as that arising from a very serious and longlasting wound would also suffice. On the other hand, even grave inconvenience and pain such as that flowing from medical treatment or an operation would not constitute sufficient "danger" to excuse one from removing the physical condition which impedes sexual intercourse.[30] Thus he strikes a balance in describing the amount of danger sufficient to constitute the impediment: it must be a real, serious danger of death, or at least of very serious illness; it cannot be mere inconvenience, yet it does not have to be death itself.

Sanchez again follows the path blazed by Soto and systematically explains this position clearly and coherently. First, he rejects the very strict interpretation of Innocent that danger means death itself. Then he cites the opinion that it could mean danger of a serious illness, — a probable danger to life. Certain authors had interpreted "periculum corporale" as not only danger to life itself, but a probable danger to life such as would be involved in a case of serious illness.[31] Soto, himself, seems to have favored this interpretation. Sanchez seems to reject this meaning of "periculum corporale": he admits that it is a probable interpretation, but argues that the more probable meaning is that given by Innocent himself: " . . . ut ex ea mortis

---

[29] INNOCENT IV, *Commentaria in V libros decretalium*, lib. IV, tit. 15, c. 6, p. 570, n. 1: " . . . sed expone, id est absque morte. Quasi dicat si mors non fuerit subsecuta ex medicamine, semper restituenda est primo viro, et hoc innuit quod sequitur 'per hoc tam gravis, ut ex ea mortis periculum.' "; IOANNIS ANDREAE, *In IV decretalium librum novella commentaria*, lib. IV, tit. 15, c. 6, p. 51, n. 26, agrees with Innocent IV's interpretation and cites Hostiensis as also agreeing with this. PANORMITANUS, *Commentaria is libros decretalium*, VII, lib. IV, rubrica *de frigidis*, c. 6, p. 61, n. 19, mentions this interpretation but rejects it.

[30] SOTO, *In Quartum Sententiarum*, II, dist. 34, q. 1, art. 2, p. 246: "Tenet, inquam, pati molestiam aliquam, et dolorem, et gravem . . ." "At gravissimum morbi incommodum non tenet perpati, praesertim cum periculo magnae lesionis, maxime si diuturna timeretur." "Quando vero citra periculum mortis curari non potest, impedimentum reputetur perpetuum: atqui: adeo dirimens."

[31] HENRIQUEZ, *Summae theoolgiae moralis*, I, lib. 12, c. 7, p. 724, n. 6: " . . . sine probabili periculo vitae aut gravis et perpetui morbi . . ."

periculum timeatur." Yet, after making this point, he, in effect, adopts just such an interpretation by declaring that there is no real difference between danger of death and danger of grave illness because the latter almost always includes the former.[32] Later on, he explicitly holds the same balanced position referred to by Soto: the danger which constitutes the impediment must be a real danger of death, or of very serious illness; mere inconvenience or pain does not constitute such danger.[33]

Subsequent authors, no doubt influenced by the authority of Sanchez, repeat that "periculum corporale" should be interpreted as danger of death, but then go on to use Sanchez' argument that danger of grave illness is, in effect, equivalent to danger of death.[34]

In conclusion, the common teaching of the canonists and theologians is: the impediment of impotence is perpetual if the only remedy for the physical condition would involve danger of death or of grave illness; pain and inconvenience would not be sufficient to constitute such danger.

---

[32] SANCHEZ, *Disputationum de sancto matrimonii sacramento*, II, lib. 7, disp. 93, p. 342, n. 16-17, and p. 343, n. 18.

[33] *Ibid.*, p. 344, n. 32: "Sed placet media via, nimirum teneri pati incisionem illam cum molestia, et gravi dolore et cauterio faciendam, at gravissimum morbi incommodum non teneri perpati."

[34] IOANNIS GUTIERREZ, *Canonicae quaestiones tam ad sponsalia de futuro quam matrimonia, eorumque impedimenta pertinentes* (Venetiis, 1618), c. 92, p. 306, n. 28 compared to p. 307, n. 31; CASTRO PALAO, *Opus morale, de virtutibus et vitiis contrariis*, Pars 5ª, tract. 28, disp. 4, punct. 14, p. 162, n. 4; BARBOSA, *Collectanea doctorum in ius pontificum universum*, II, lib. IV, tit. 15, p. 564, n. 13; PEREZ ab UNANOA, *Opus morale theologicum de sancto matrimonii sacramento*, disp. 37, sect. 1, p. 409, n. 3: "Et ratio est, quia tametsi id quod absque morte auferri potest, non sit physice perpetuum; si tamen non possit absque periculo mortis, est moraliter perpetuum: nam periculum mortis moraliter aequivalet morti. ...Quod autem auferri nequit absque gravi et perpetuo morbo, censetur perpetuum: quia iste aequivalet moraliter morti physicae, non minus, imo magis quam periculum mortis..."; REIFFENSTUEL, *Ius canonicum universum*, IV, lib. IV, tit. 15, p. 120, n. 66, compared with p. 115, n. 7; RONCAGLIA, *Universa moralis theologia*, tom. 2, tract. 21, q. 4, c. 6, p. 203, compared with p. 202; ALPHONSUS DE LIGUORI, *Theologia moralis*, lib. 6, tract. 6, cap. 3, dub. 2, p. 227, n. 1097. Authors who deny that danger of grave illness constitutes the impediment are: SCHMIER, *Iurisprudentia canonico-civilis seu ius canonicum universum*, III, lib. 4, tract. 3, cap. 2, sect. 2, p. 107, n. 81; SCHMALZGRUEBER, *Ius ecclesiasticum universum*, tom. IV, pars 3, tit. 15, p. 153, n. 4; VITUS PICHLER, *Ius canonicum secundum quinque decretalium titulos*, II (Pisauri, ²1758), lib. 4, tit. 15, p. 504.

c) *Controversy over the Obligation to Remove an Impotent Condition If There Is No Danger of Death or Serious Illness Involved*

The starting point for the above discussion, which determined the amount of danger necessary to constitute the impediment, was a very practical problem: Does a woman with an impenetrable hymen have an obligation to remove this condition, if it can be done without any danger? In an attempt to answer this question, the authors we dealt with in the previous section were led to distinguish the various amounts of permissible pain, discomfort and danger which would, in their opinion, constitute the impediment as perpetual or temporary. Their conclusions as to the presence or absence of the obligation do not directly interest the question of perpetuity. Much more important for our inquiry is the process by which they reached their conclusions. Whether they realized it or not, these authors had a *standard*, a principle, a measuring rod which they used in order to come to a decision. That standard, that principle, that measuring rod, seems to be the notion of ordinary and extraordinary means. The decisions made above about the amount of danger necessary to constitute the impediment were really decisions as to whether or not this particular cure, this particular operation would be an ordinary or extraordinary means to accomplish the ends of marriage. They were deciding whether a particular action was morally possible or impossible for the average person.

The conclusion that serious danger of death or grave illness constituted the impediment was a judgment that removal of the physical condition under these circumstances would be something morally impossible for the average man to endure. The conclusion that pain or inconvenience did *not* constitute the impediment was a judgment that removal of the physical condition in those circumstances would be something ordinary and morally possible for the average person to undergo.

Several authors give definite indications that they reasoned in this manner. De Coninck defines temporary impotence as that which can be removed by *ordinary* human means.[35]

Castro Palao denies that a virgin would have to endure an operation to remedy a merely natural condition such as an

---

[35] DE CONINCK, *De sacramentis et censuris*, II, disp. 31, dub. 7, p. 812, n. 76.

impenetrable hymen: he reasons that the opening of the hymen by any means other than that of normal sexual intercourse would be something totally extraordinary. Consequently, the woman would have no obligation to submit to such a "cure," the impediment would be permanent and the marriage invalid.[36]

Perez ab Unanoa does conclude that the woman would be obliged to submit to the operation in those circumstances, even after reporting the opinions of Petrus de Ledesma and Gaspar Hurtado who state that she is obliged to use only ordinary and *not* extraordinary means to fulfill the marriage contract. The importance of this passage is not the conclusion reached but rather the fact that Perez does not reject the opinion cited, rather he embraces it: he simply has a different judgment as to what concretely is an ordinary or extraordinary means.[37]

The Theologians of Salamanca together with Tournely seem to favor the opinion that the woman would not be obliged to submit to the operation since it is something almost morally impossible to require of anyone.[38]

---

[36] CASTRO PALAO, *Opus morale, de virtutibus et vitiis contrariis*, tract. 28, disp. 4, punct. 14, p. 162, n. 8: "Moveor, quia coniunx in matrimonio corpus suum alteri coniugi tradit ad usum coniugalem, prout a natura destinatum est, at natura non destinavit aperitionem claustri virginalis in ordine ad coniugalem usum fieri deberi alio medio quam viri pudendo, *quinimmo omnem alium modum utpote extraordinarium natura abhorret, ergo non tenetur* foemina illo uti." (Emphasis mine).

[37] PEREZ ab UNANOA, *Opus morale theologicum de sancto matrimonii sacramento*, disp. 37, sect. 1, p. 415, n. 6 and n. 8: "...nam virginem artificio aperiri in bonum usum matrimonii decens est, et conforme naturae, et in obsequium viri iam sui, cui enim est vinculo matrimonii astricta. Quae enim turpitudo, vel indecentia in ea actione necessaria, et ordinata ad finem matrimonii iam contracti ex iure exequendum, inveniri vel excogitari potest." See also, Alphonsus de Liguori as quoted in footnote 25 of this chapter.

[38] SALMANTICENSES, *Cursus theologiae moralis*, II, tract. 9, c. 12, punct. 10, p. 161, n. 116, temper their previous assertion that she must undergo the operation by noting: "Aliqui temperant, nisi morbus esset gravissimus, et laesio magna, et diuturna: quia durissimum esset aliquam cum tanto incommodo ad copulam matrimonii obligare."; TOURNELY, see footnote 25 of this chapter; cf. RONCAGLIA, *Universa moralis theologia*, tom. 2, tract. 21, q. 4, c. 6, p. 204; ALPHONSUS DE LIGUORI, *Theologia moralis*, lib. 6, tract. 6, cap. 3, dub. 2, p. 228, n. 1099: "...quod esset onus plus quam gravissimum..."

## B. THE NOTION OF ORDINARY AND EXTRAORDINARY MEANS

It seems quite clear from our historical investigation of the content of the concept of perpetuity that the authors used a standard by which they judged the presence or absence of sufficient danger; that standard was the concept of ordinary and extraordinary means. The judgment about the sufficiency of the danger was likewise a decision that the impediment was perpetual; the determination of the perpetuity of the impediment was at the same time a decision about the invalidity of the marriage. In brief, the determination of the sufficiency of danger, in effect, determined the impediment — the incompatibility of this concrete situation with the ends of marriage. Thus the whole process of decision-making was dependent on the standard of ordinary and extraordinary means.

Yet in Chapter Two (see p. 63), it had appeared that the concept of perpetuity itself was the quality, the specification, the standard by which one judged the incompatibility of a particular situation with the ends of marriage. What, then, is the relationship between the concept of perpetuity and the concept of ordinary and extraordinary means? Before being able to compare them we must first have a clear understanding of the notion of ordinary and extraordinary means which has been a part of moral theology as far back as the period we have been discussing.

### 1. *The Classical Doctrine*

Moral theologians appear to have developed what is now known as the concept of ordinary and extraordinary means in their treatises on the Fifth Commandment where they deal with the duty one has to safeguard and preserve his life. Quite naturally, authors concerned with medical ethics have been in the forefront of those studying and clarifying this concept. As a result, these authors have been more concerned with establishing a practical definition of ordinary and extraordinary means for doctors to use in actual medical situations rather than speculating about what ordinariness or extraordinariness consists in. Thus there is at least an extrinsic similarity between this concept and that of perpetuity; the concept of perpetuity also evolved from an attempt to answer a concrete particular problem, that which had been presented to Innocent III.

The moralists use copious examples to illustrate what they mean by ordinary and extraordinary means. From these examples we can conclude that an ordinary means is one that is proportionate, congruent, ordered to the end that is to be attained.[39] It is also one that is commonly available, at hand, and which presents no great difficulty to use.[40]

The notion of extraordinary means is correlative to that of ordinary; it is its negative, its opposite. Our remarks will be limited to extraordinary from here on, but they will thus apply also to ordinary means, in a negative sense.

In spite of this correlativity, authors seem to have slightly more difficulty in expressing what constitutes an extraordinary means of preserving one's life. Amputation of hand or foot, or any other major operation is considered extraordinary because it is too difficult, too painful.[41] Other types of extraordinary means would be: moving away from home for reasons

---

[39] FRANCISCUS DE VICTORIA, *Relectionum theologicarum*, II: *Relectio de homicidio*, (Lugduni, 1557) p. 148, n. 35, photo-offset in *Relecciones teológicas del Maestro Fray Francisco de Vitoria*, ed. Luis G. Alonso-Getino, III, (Madrid, 1935) pp. 24-38; Dominicus Banes, *Decisiones de iure et iustitia*, IV (Duaci, [4]1615), q. 65, art. 1, pp. 204-205; Eduardus Genicot, *Theologiae moralis Institutiones*, I (Lovanii, [3]1900), p. 345, n. 364; Ioseph AERTNYS-C. DAMEN, *Theologia moralis*, ed. J. Visser (Italia, [17]1956), p. 528, n. 566.

[40] BONACINA, *Opera omnia*, II: *De legibus deque Decalogi et Ecclesiae praeceptis* (Venetiis, 1728), disp. 2, q. ult., punc. 6, p. 453: "... remediis ordinariis non valde difficilibus..."; LEONARDUS LESSIUS, *De iustitia et iure* (Lugduni, 1622), lib. 2, cap. 9, dub. 14, p. 101, n. 96: "... mediis ordinariis non admodum difficilibus..."; LAYMANN, *Theologia moralis*, lib. 3, tract. 3, pars 3, cap. 1, p. 274, n. 4: "... medium valde difficile et insolitum..."; IOANNIS DE LUGO, *De iustitia et iure*, I (Lugduni, 1642), disp. 10, sect. 1, n. 21: "... non tenetur homo media extraordinaria et difficillima adhibere... sed ordinaria et non admodum difficilia..."; BANES, *Decisiones de iure et iustitia*, IV, q. 65, art. 1, p. 205; ALPHONSUS DE LIGUORI, *Theologia moralis*, I, lib. 3, n. 372: "... non teneri quemquam mediis extraordinariis et nimis duris,..."

[41] BANES, *Decisiones de iure et iustitia*, IV, q. 65, art. 1, p. 205: "... per medicinas communes, per dolorem quemdam communem et ordinarium: non tamen per quemdam dolorem extraordinarios, secundum proportionem status ipsius hominis."; TOURNELY, *De universa theologia moralis*, III, *de 5° praecepto*, c. 2, concl. 2, s. v. *quartus casus*, p. 425; RONCAGLIA, *Universa moralis theologia*, tract. 11, q. 1, c. 1, p. 362. See also, Lessius, De Lugo and Bonacina in the places cited in footnote 40 of this chapter.

of health, very expensive treatments or medicines.[42]  Franciscus
de Victoria, reflecting the Mediterranean world with which he
was familiar, goes so far as to say that to be required to perpetually abstain from wine would be an extraordinary means
of preserving one's life! [43]  There is no doubt that the authors
teach that certain apparently subjective elements such as pain,
horror, embarrassment also contribute to constituting an operation or treatment as an extraordinary means.[44]

So many examples are given, so many circumstances considered, so many contradictory opinions voiced, that it does not
seem possible to arrive at a clear understanding of just what
an extraordinary means is.

Perhaps a speculative, philosophical reflection will help at
this point.

## 2. *Philosophical Reflection*

In the physical order, a means, considered statically, is
something equidistant from a *terminus a quo* and a *terminus
ad quem*; dynamically, it is an instrument by which one goes
from one *terminus* to another.  Hence it is always in relation
to these *termini*; it is a relative term.  In the noëtical order of
the intellect and will, means also refers to a relation or relationship.  In the moral order, understood here as the order of the
will seeking goods or ends (ultimately its final good, its final
end), a means is an intermediate end.[45]

---

[42] Change of climate as an extraordinary means is mentioned by
JOSEPH UBACH, *Theologia moralis*, I (Bonis Auris, [2]1935), p. 286; also,
H. NOLDIN-A. SCHMITT, *Summa theologiae moralis*, II: *De praeceptis Dei
et Ecclesiae* (Oeniponte/Lipsiae, [27]1941), p. 307, n. 325.  Expensive medicines or treatments are mentioned by Banes, Roncaglia and Tourneiy
in the places just cited in the previous footnote.

[43] DE VICTORIA, *Relectionum theologicarum*, II, p. 148, n. 34.

[44] For pain, see Banes, Lessius, De Lugo, Bonacina, in the places cited
in footnote 40 of this chapter; for horror, see EDUARDUS GENICOT, *Theologiae moralis Institutiones*, I, p. 345, n. 364; UBACH, *Theologia moralis*, I,
p. 286, n. 488; for embarassment, see RONCAGLIA, *Universa moralis theologia*, tract. 11, q. 1 c. 1, p. 362; ALPHONSUS DE LIGUORI, *Theologia moralis*,
I, lib. 3, n. 372; UBACH, *Theologia moralis*, p. 286, n. 487.

[45] For the exact sense in which we use moral order in this sentence,
see JOHN FORD, *The Validity of Virginal Marriage* (Dissertation submitted
to the Pontificia Universitas Gregoriana) (Worcester, Mass., 1938), pp.
44-45.  Also, see THOMAS O'DONNELL, *Morals in Medicine* (Westminster,
Md., [2]1959), pp. 9-10; P. G. PAYEN, *Déontologie médicale d'après le droit
natural* (Zi-ka-wei [Chang-Hai], 1935), pp. 6-7.

The moralists spoken of earlier establish the principle that one is obliged only to use ordinary means to preserve his life; one does not have to use difficult or inconvenient means.[46] Lessius hints at the real explanation for this by referring to Aquinas' *Supplementum*, q. 65, art. 1, resp.[47]  Here St. Thomas describes the operation of the will seeking its end as a natural process, a kind of natural law.  Everything that makes the attaining of the end inconvenient, everything that blocks, disturbs or interferes with the attainment of the end is in a certain sense against the law of nature.

But something can interfere with the attainment of the end in two ways: 1) either by completely blocking the accomplishment of the end, or 2) by making it unpleasant or difficult to attain the end.  If something completely interferes with the attainment of the end, the natural law itself forbids one to use that means to attain the end.  If a means merely makes it difficult or inconvenient to attain the end, one is not absolutely forbidden to use that means but the secondary precepts of the natural law (speculative principles) admonish and dissuade one from using that means to attain the end.  One *could* use that means, but in a certain sense such a use would be contrary to the natural law because reason sees that such a means is inconvenient, incongruent, disproportionate to the end.[48]

If we examine once more the examples given by the moralists in the light of the above, we see that the same situation is presented: there is an end to be attained (saving and preserving one's life) and a concrete set of circumstances.  We are trying to abstract from all these examples that which they have in common, — "extraordinariness."  In the expression "extraordinary means," extraordinary is an adjective qualifying means.

---

[46] See footnotes 40 and 41 of this chapter.

[47] LESSIUS, *De iustitia et iure,* lib. 2, c. 9, dub. 14, p. 101, n. 96.

[48] THOMAS AQUINAS, *Supplementum Tertiae Partis Summae Theologicae,* q. 65, art. 1, resp.: "Omne autem illud quod actionem inconvenientem reddit fini quem natura ex opere aliquo intendit, contra legem naturae esse dicitur.  Potest autem actio non esse conveniens fini ... dupliciter.  Uno modo, ex aliquo quod omnino impedit finem. ... Alio modo, ex aliquo quod facit difficilem vel minus decentem perventionem ad finem. ... Et sic dicta actio contra legem naturae esse dicitur."  O'DONNELL, *Morals in Medicine,* p. 21, points out the qualities a law must have: right order must be preserved, the law must be useful, and it must be possible of observance.  If the analogy used by St. Thomas is correct, then an extraordinary means will lack these qualities.  It will become clear below that an extraordinary means does lack just such qualities.

The abstract notion, extraordinariness, is therefore a quality, a mode of the relationship of a set of concrete circumstances to an end.

Extraordinariness is in fact the quality of disproportionality present in the relationship of these circumstances to that particular end.[49] It is determined by a practical judgment of right reason in the light of the value of the end and the necessity of attaining it . We can, therefore, conclude that an extraordinary means is one that is disproportionate to the end; it is one which entails a certain incapacity, incongruence, inconvenience in attaining the end. Such a disproportion does not always prohibit, but does dissuade one from using the means. Certainly, one could never be required or obliged to use that means because it is naturally disproportionate, incongruous, incompatible with the end.

### 3. *Distinctive Characteristic of Extraordinary Means*: *No Obligation to Use It*

From our above reflection it would seem that that which makes a means extraordinary is right reason's judgment that there is an inconvenience, a disproportion in the use of this means. The disproportion or inconvenience is such that it does not completely prohibit the use of the means, but it removes any obligation to use that means.

Most moralists, but especially the modern ones, have seen this non-obligatory element as the distinctive characteristic of an extraordinary means. Edwin Healy writes:

---

[49] The following authors show that they considered a certain disproportionality to be fundamental to every extraordinary means: BANES, *Decisiones de iure et iustitia*, q. 65, art. 1, p. 204: "... quia tenetur servare vitam per media ordinata et proportionata: sed abscissio membri est medium proportionatum." AERTNYS-DAMEN, *Theologia moralis*, p. 528, n. 566: "Unusquisque tenetur vitam et corpus suam conservare ac perficere mediis ordinariis *in ordine ad finem suum consequendum.*" (Emphasis mine); EDWIN HEALY, *Medical Ethics* (Chicago, 1956, p. 65: "... there must be present a just proportion between the good effects which presumably will follow and the inconveniences and difficulties attendant upon the use of the measures in question."; *ibid.*, p. 67: "We may here define as an extraordinary means whatever here and now is very costly, or very unusual or very painful or very difficult, or very dangerous, *or if the good effects that can be expected from its use are not proportionate to the difficulty and inconvenience that are entailed.*" (Emphasis mine); see also O'DONNELL, *Morals in Medicine*, p. 32.

Men in general do not possess the energy or the fortitude to employ extraordinary measures to preserve their life. The obligation to preserve life by means that are very painful or very difficult to obtain would be regarded by the generality of mankind as an intolerable burden and as an exorbitant and unproportionate price to pay for the benefit gained. No one can be under the obligation of doing what is impossible. An act may be impossible in one of two ways, either physically or morally. It is physically impossible when one has not at his command the physical means of performing the action. It would, for example, be physically impossible for a blind man to read by using his eyes. An act is called morally impossible if its performance would overtax the will power and courage of the normal person. It is clear, therefore, that God does not oblige us to use such means in order to survive; but we are at liberty to use them if we can and if we so desire. There is nothing that forbids our using extraordinary measures to conserve or to regain our health. [50]

Charles McFadden succinctly synthesizes the general feeling of the moral theologians: " It is of the very nature of an extraordinary means that, outside of the two exceptions stated earlier, there is no obligation to use it." [51]

## 4. *The Situation of Moral Impossibility*

From what has been said so far it seems that we can conclude that an extraordinary means is one which involves disproportion to the end so that right reason would say that one is not held to use that means. This is a general principle valid for any extraordinary means. Yet, it does not seem to be quite

---

[50] HEALY, *Medical Ethics*, p. 61.

[51] CHARLES MCFADDEN, *Medical Ethics* (Philadelphia, [4]1956), p. 265. The following authors all recognize the special non-obligatory characteristic of an extraordinary means: Victoria, Banes, Bonacina, Lessius, Laymann, de Lugo, Alphonsus de Liguori, Roncaglia, Tournely, Genicot, Aertnys-Damen, Ubach, Noldin-Schmitt in the places cited in footnotes 39-42 of this chapter. To these can be added: A. BALLERINI-B. PALMIERI, *Opus theologicum morale*, II (Prati, [3]1899), p. 632, n. 855; GERALD KELLY, "The Duty of Using Artificial Means of Preserving Life, "*Theological Studies*, 11 (1950), p. 206. For the Rotal jurisprudence, see c. FELICI, 10 July 1959, *Dec.* 51, p. 378, n. 6; c. PINNA, 2 March 1958, *Dec.* 50, p. 201, n. 2: "... agi de medio extraordinario quo nemo uti tenetur,"; c. DI FELICE, 28 November 1968, *ME* 94 (1969), 102.

exact. McFadden as quoted above, himself makes two exceptions to his general principle.

The matter can be clarified by realizing that we have defined as extraordinary any means that is disproportionate to the end. The classical authors as well as the modern have limited their notion of extraordinary means to one situation, the situation of moral impossibility. For all practical purposes when we speak of extraordinary means we are speaking of a means in this context of moral impossibility. Hence an extraordinary means, *properly so called*, involves moral impossibility.

Many hypothetical situations can be imagined in the moral, intentional order of the will seeking ends which we have referred to earlier (see footnotes 45 and 48 of this chapter). In a broad sense, anything which right reason would see as out of proportion to the end, too difficult or too inconvenient would be an extraordinary means of attaining that end. When faced with such a situation the will could abandon the end, choose a multiplicity of other means to attain the end, or decide to use this means notwithstanding the difficulty involved.

A morally impossible situation arises, however, in a hypothesis where the end must be attained and there are *no* other means available. The obligation to attain the end arises either from the fact that this end is in itself merely an intermediate end to something further and hence cannot be abandoned, or from some obligation of law or duty. This situation gives rise to a moral impossibility because the end cannot be abandoned, nor can it be attained without requiring one to do more than his duty, more than his moral capability. Hence it is morally impossible to attain the end, because the will cannot be *required* to use a means which right reason has judged disproportionate and extraordinary. O'Donnell defines obligation as: moral necessity superimposed upon the physical freedom of the human will directing free actions according to right order.[52] Hence it is quite evident that there can be no obligation, no moral necessity directing free actions according to right order, in a situation in which right reason judges that right order and due proportion are lacking.

O'Donnell clearly describes what this moral impossibility is:

---

[52] O'DONNELL, *Morals in Medicine*, p. 22.

Moral impossibility does not mean actual impossibility in the ordinary sense of the word, but refers to those circumstances in which observance of the law would demand something like "heroism beyond the call of duty." Moral impossibility excuses from the observance of any law except the negative precepts of the natural law. [53]

... the effort required to constitute moral impossibility, which might range in a particular case from grave inconvenience to heroism, is to be judged in proportion to the importance of the law, i.e. the good to be achieved by its observance. [54]

A similar definition of moral impossibility is given by Roberti-Palazzini: A moral impossibility is a difficulty that allows the physical fulfillment of a obligation but renders it extraordinarily burdensome. There is no duty to fulfill an obligation when it gives rise to a situation of moral impossibility. There can be different grades of moral impossibility in proportion to the importance of the end and the necessity to attain it; the highest level of moral impossibility is had when that which one would be obliged to do has itself become morally illicit; in that case one would not merely be permitted but would be required to omit the action.[55]

Roberti-Palazzini add a very important cautionary note: one must remenber that the juridic and the moral orders are correlative but not exactly coextensive. The moral order is responsible to the natural law judged by the practical norm of right reason (conscience); the juridic order depends on the norms of human positive law. Moral impossibility, properly speaking, is in the moral order; the same phenomenon in the juridic order is an excusing cause.[56]

As a conclusion of this study of moral impossibility we can state an important principle: one *can* physically *do* the morally impossible, but ONE CAN NEVER BE OBLIGED TO DO THE MORALLY IMPOSSIBLE.

---

[53] *Ibid.*, p. 32.

[54] *Ibid.*, p. 33.

[55] F. ROBERTI-P. PALAZZINI, *Dizionario di teologia morale*, I (Roma, ⁴1968), s. v. *impossibilità*. See also GOMMARUS MICHIELS, *Normae generales iuris canonici*, I (Parisiis-Tornaci-Romae, ²1949), 463. Michiels calls this highest level of moral impossibility "impotentia absoluta ordinis spiritualis." See also VAN HOVE, *De legibus ecclesiasticis*, I (Mechlinae-Romae, 1930), 298, n. 290.

[56] ROBERTI-PALAZZINI, *Dizionario di teologia morale*, s. v. *causa scusante*. See also, c. BONET, 22 December 1960, Dec. 52, p. 607, n. 17.

## 5. *Relative Characteristic of an Extraordinary Means*

Several objections could be raised against the descriptive definition that we have given of extraordinary means. Since an extraordinary means, *properly* so called, gives rise to a moral impossibility, it follows that one could *never* be required to do the extraordinary, never be required to make use of the extraordinary means. Yet such a statement does not seem to be justified because the moralists, though recognizing the non-obligatory characteristic of an extraordinary means, are usually careful to limit this by the words "generally," "usually," or by the distinctions *per se* and *per accidens*.[57] Healy quite clearly states: "Under certain circumstances one might be obliged to use extraordinary means."[58] Furthermore, the term morally impossible could be confusing; somehow it does not just seem right to say that one *can do* the impossible, even if it is only the morally impossible.

Before being able to clarify these points and justify the terminology chosen, it is necessary to be aware of a unique aspect of the problem which is the source of much confusion in establishing a clear, univocal meaning for the idea of extraordinary means. That aspect is the relativity of the notion.

As far back as Banes, the moralists had mentioned that an extraordinary means could only be defined in relation to the individual in his concrete circumstances.[59] Genicot, too, says that a person must use means that are ordinary and in accord

---

[57] DE LUGO, *De iustitia et iure*, I, disp. 10, sec. 1, n. 21: "...nisi forte ea sit persona cuius vita bono publico sit valde necessaria."; LAYMANN, *Theologia moralis*, lib. 3, tract. 3, pars 3, c. 1, p. 274, n. 4: "plerumque ...non tenemur"; TOURNELY, *De universa theologia moralis*, III, *de 5° praecepto*, c. 2, concl. 2, s. v. *quartus casus*, p. 425; ALPHONSUS DE LIGUORI, *Theologia moralis*, I, lib. 3, n. 372: "...nisi tamen ea communi bono sit necessaria."; GENICOT, *Theologiae moralis Institutiones*, I, p. 345, n. 364: "per accidens"; BALLERINI-PALMIERI, *Opus theologicum morale*, II, p. 632, n. 855; NOLDIN-SCHMITT, *Summa theologiae moralis*, II, p. 307, n. 325: "per se"; KELLY, "The Duty of Using Artificial Means of Preserving Life," p. 206: "*per se, per accidens*"; McFADDEN, *Medical Ethics*, p. 280; JOHN GOODWINE [discussion leader], "The Physician's Duty to Preserve Life by Extraordinary Means," *Proceedings of the Catholic Theological Society*, 7 (1952), 125-138: "*per se, per accidens*."

[58] HEALY, *Medical Ethics*, p. 68.

[59] BANES, *Decisiones de iure et iustitia*, IV, q. 65, ast. 1, p. 205: "...secundum proportionem status ipsius hominis."

with his position in life.[60]  Ubach says the same thing in another way when he points out that the extraordinariness of the means has to be determined by the circumstances of the individual.  Thus for a Carthusian monk who has vowed perpetual abstinence, eating meat which is necessary to save his life could be considered an extraordinary means.  For a virgin who would rather suffer death than embarrassment, an operation on the genital organs could also be considered an extraordinary means.[61]

The notion of extraordinary means seems purely relative. Not only is it determined by accidental circumstances such as wealth, distance from a doctor, the state of medical knowledge in one's country, but even by apparently subjective elements. Kelly reports: "However, some of these authors readily admit the possibility of a subjective repugnance which would make the operations extraordinary means for certain individuals." [62]

The notion of extraordinary means is thus so relative that an *ordinary* means can be an *extraordinary* means, and an *extraordinary* means can be an *ordinary* one — all depending on the circumstances and the individual.[63]

The above problem was not of immediate concern to the authors dealing with the notion of extraordinary means because they were not trying to determine a speculative definition of extraordinariness, but rather to give a practical rule of thumb to doctors.  Nonetheless, the conflicting notions of or-

---

[60] GENICOT, *Theologiae moralis Institutiones*, I, p. 345, n. 364: "...mediis ordinariis et statui suo congruentibus...."

[61] UBACH, *Theologia moralis*, n. 487: "Sic multi excusant, immo laudabant monachum Carthusianum qui in gravi morbi nollet vesci carnibus, quibus sanitatem recuperare posset; valde enim ad bonum Ordinis confert, ut regula abstinentiae perpetuae etiam cum vitae discrimine servetur.  Non tenetur virgo subire manus medici vel chirurgi, si id ei gravissimum est et magis horret quam ipsam mortem...."

[62] KELLY, "The Duty of Using Artificial Means of Preserving Life," p. 205.

[63] UBACH, *Theologia moralis*, I, n. 487: "In quibusdam circumstantiis potest aliquod *medium ex se ordinarium, censeri extraordinarium...*" (Emphasis mine); JULES PAQUIN, *Morale et médecine* (Montreal, 1955), p. 399: "...ainsi *une remède ordinaire* pour la plupart des gens *peut devenir extraordinaire*, parceque trop couteux, pour une personne extremement pauvre...: ainsi encore, *un traitement ordinaire en lui-même*, mais pour lequel le malade a une extrème repugnance, *sera* peut-être *pour lui en moyen extraordinaire*." (Emphasis mine); *ibid.*, p. 400: "Le tout est à juger moralement, en tenant compte de bien des circonstances."

dinary and extraordinary led certain authors to attempt to address this problem. They began to ask: Is the distinction between ordinary and extraordinary purely relative, or is there an absolute norm beyond which a means must be considered extraordinary? [64] Their immediate attention was devoted to the question of the expense of the treatment as a circumstance affecting extraordinariness. Healy speaks of an absolute and a relative norm for determining what would be an extraordinary treatment. An absolute norm is that beyond which no one need go in spending money to care for his health. This norm is based on that which people in general would find very costly. He sets a figure of $2,000.00 or more as this absolute norm. The relative norm would take into consideration an individual in particular, unusual circumstances — a very rich man for example. For such a man more than $2,000 would not be extraordinary. [65]

Later authors find fault with trying to establish a monetary figure as an absolute limit; such a limit would have to be constantly changed and thus serves no purpose.

O'Donnell, in our opinion, finds the key to the solution of this problem by noting that the relativity in trying to distinguish ordinary and extraordinary means is really the relation of due proportion. In order to determine what is ordinary and extraordinary in the preservation of life one must judge the proportion between the cost and effort required to preserve the fundamental context (of the goods of human life) and the potentialities of the other goods that still remain to be worked out within that context. [66] This answer does not define ordinary and extraordinary means in a practical definite way but provides the ultimate grounds for the necessary moral judgment. For this reason it seems to be, in essence, the same position presented above in our philosophical reflection.

Thus we can say that the notion of ordinary and extraordinary means is relative, but it is not purely relative. It is determined by a practical moral judgment of the relationship

---

[64] KELLY, "The Duty of Using Artificial Means of Preserving Life," p. 206. See also F. HERVADA, *La impotencia del varon nel derecho canonico* (Pamplona, 1959), p. 224: "...la calificacion de ordinario o extraordinario de un medio debe hacerse dentro de unas mismas condiciones ambientales en relacion al caso general o al caso concreto?"

[65] HEALY, *Medical Ethics*, pp. 67-68.

[66] O'DONNELL, *Morals in Medicine*, pp. 71-72.

of a set of circumstances to a goal or end. If it would be disproportionate, too inconvenient or beyond the resources of the average man to use a certain means to attain the end, then that means is extraordinary. Relativity enters in, insofar as the goal, the circumstances or even the norm of judgment can change, thereby changing the proportional relationship.

The attempt to determine extraordinariness can be compared to trying to weigh something on an old-fashioned balance scale: on the one side we have the goal plus all the concrete circumstances, on the other we have the norm of the common man, the generality of mankind as mentioned by Healy. If the scale is in balance, the means will be ordinary; if there is an imbalance, the means will be extraordinary. The proportion and the result will change any time I change one of the circumstances, or if I change the goal. For example, the circumstances are: a man is dying and needs an operation, the goal is to save and preserve life. All things considered, we would say that should a surgical operation be chosen as the means, such a means would be ordinary. If we add the circumstance that the operation requires a very rare and skilled doctor, we now see a disproportion that tips the scale to make this an extraordinary means. Thus even though there be relativity, once a definite goal and definite circumstances have been weighed against a definite norm, one can always come up with an objective judgment whether this means is extraordinary or not.

One could object that there is still another element of relativity, — relativity to the individual. If we use the example of expense, the above ordinary operation might still be beyond the resources of a very poor man, although quite within the budget of the average man. Thus it would be an ordinary means, but extraordinary for the poor man.

Our response would be to point out that in presenting the example in this way, the objector has changed part of the balance. He has not added a new goal, nor even a new circumstance — but he has changed the norm, the other side of the balance. He has substituted the norm of the individual in the place of the average man. Thus the scale is correct, because it shows that this operation is still an extraordinary means for this particular individual. Rather than say ordinary has become extraordinary, let us recognize that we have changed the norm; according to this norm the operation *was* and *is* extraordinary.

Our conclusion is that the notion of the extraordinary means is a relative notion, but it is not purely relative. There is an objective standard that an impartial observer can use; that standard is the proportion or disproportion involved in using this means to that end in these circumstances. Extraordinariness can thus be defined as a quality of a means (the relationship of a concrete set of circumstances to an end) consisting in a disproportion freeing one from any obligation to use that means.

In our opinion, part of this confusion about the notion of ordinary and extraordinary is due to defective terminology. The earlier moral theologians gave their examples of extraordinariness based on the norm of the average man, the *vir prudens*. They were establishing general principles and using the *theoretical figure of the common man as their standard of judgment*. The recent medical ethicians approach the problem from the basis of questions arising in actual medical practice; these concern *actual individuals* in *actual* concrete *circumstances*. Thus many of these means in actual circumstances are extraordinary, though according to theory they are only ordinary. The terminology, *per se, per accidens*, or even *relative* and *absolute* extraordinary means, does not bring out clearly enough the fact that there is a complete change in the norm of evaluation when one goes from a *per se* ordinary to a *per accidens* ordinary means, or from an *absolute* to a *relative* ordinary means. Even the terms *objectively* and *subjectively* ordinary means are not adequate because they give the impression that subjectively extraordinary means are not really extraordinary, because they seem to depend on subjective factors in the mind of the individual rather than on objective reality. Such an impression would be totally unjustified because the determination of extraordinariness is not left to the will of the individual, but is determined by measurement against the norm of the average person, or the norm of the individual in his concrete situation.

The proper terminology, in our opinion, would be *theoretically ordinary* means as distinguished from *actually ordinary* means. Such a distinction is hinted at by McFadden: "Personally, in evaluating this problem, I should like to distinguish between this case considered *theoretically* as contrasted with the case in *actual* medical practice." [67]

---

[67] McFADDEN, *Medical Ethics*, p. 272.

Such a terminology would clearly indicate whether we are dealing with the notion on the abstract, general level or whether we are trying to decide a particular case involving a real individual in his existential situation. Furthermore, the shift in adjectives would clearly *alert* us to the fact that we are changing *norms of evaluation rather than objective circumstances*.

## 6. *Reply to Objections*

a) The adoption of this distinction and this terminology will allow us to respond to the objections raised earlier. It had been objected that our conclusion, that one could never be required to do the morally impossible, to make use of an extraordinary means, was not accurate because the approved authors clearly teach that in some circumstances one could be required to use extraordinary means. Our response is: the general principle that one cannot be required to use an extraordinary means holds true in all cases, *for an actually* extraordinary means. However, one *may* at some time *be required* to make use of a *theoretically* extraordinary means.

Gerald Kelly gives a set of principles governing the use of ordinary and extraordinary means. We can adopt these principles exactly if we delete the distinctions *per se* and *per accidens*, and add the adjective *theoretical* and *actual*. Thus:

1. An individual is obliged to use ordinary means to preserve his life.
2. He is not obliged to use extraordinary means.
3. However, he can at some time be obliged to use *theoretically* extraordinary means, if the preservation of his life is required for some greater good such as his own spiritual welfare or the common good. However, no one at any time can ever be required to use *actually* extraordinary means.[68]

By adding the distinction *theoretically* and *actually* we serve notice that two elements in the balance have changed. A circumstance of special weight (life required for his own spiritual welfare or for the common good) has been added so that the case must be judged according to the norm of the individual rather than the average man.

---

[68] Cf. KELLY, "The Duty of Using Artificial Means of Preserving Life,» p. 206.

b) With regard to the second objection: it does not seem right to say that one can do the impossible even if it is only the morally impossible. Our response is: it is even more incongruous to say that an ordinary means is sometimes extraordinary and an extraordinary means is sometimes ordinary. With the definition and terminology presented here one can always say that a means is extraordinary whenever there is a disproportion (either theoretical or actual) to the end. A situation of moral impossibility can arise from either a theoretically or an actually extraordinary means. One can *never be required* to do the morally impossible, but yet one *can* do it.

c) One may ask: Is this substitution of evaluative norms valid? Do the principles of obligation to use the means hold true in the face of this distinction between actual and theoretical? Kelly asks himself a similar question. Though his terminology and explanations differ slightly from that given above, in substance his conclusion is the same: a means is truly extraordinary and the principles are valid no matter which norm one uses. Hence he speaks of the relative norm (*actually* extraordinary means in our terms) "sufficing" to consider a means extraordinary.[69]

In our opinion, the perspective should be reversed. Most often one will be dealing with an individual case and will want to decide if the means *for this individual* in these circumstances are extraordinary or not. For the individual, an actually extraordinary means will exempt him from obligation in all cases and will be that which is truly extraordinary for him. A theoretically extraordinary means (one based on the norm of the average man) will, however, generally suffice to excuse the individual from any obligation to use that means, since a person will not normally be required to exceed the common diligence of men. Thus, as Healy would have it, an operation costing more than $2,000 will be extraordinary for both the poor and the rich man and neither could be obliged to use it. Such

---

[69] *Ibid.*, p. 206: "My general impression is that there is common agreement that a relative estimate suffices.... But is the relative inconvenience always required? Some authors clearly deny this. For instance, they say that even a wealthy man need not spend large sums of money to obtain the best doctors. Ubach explains this by saying that such means are beyond the reach of most men and that they exceed 'common diligence.' "

an operation is actually extraordinary for the poor man but only theoretically extraordinary for the rich man.

d) A further complaint might still be raised: the notion of extraordinary means presented here is not objective; it is determined by the interested party's subjective point of view. Fear, horror, embarrassment, and perception of pain are all subjective feelings; any consideration of them, any admission of them as contributing factors to the notion of extraordinary means vitiates any attempt to produce an objective definition.

Our first observation is that any decision about the ordinariness or extraordinariness of a means is a judgment made by an impartial observer. It is not the interested party, the patient, who determines if this is an extraordinary means or not. Noldin-Schmitt tell us that the judgment is left to the common estimation of men.[70] Hence the purely subjective whims or wishes of the person using the means does not determine the ordinariness or extraordinariness of those means. Such a determination is made by any informed onlooker, a judge, a doctor — anyone who is capable of making a rational judgment involving several ponderables.[71]

Secondly, it is quite true that fear, horror, embarrassment, perception of pain, and intensity of faith are all subjective elements of reality, i.e. based on personal subjective feelings or perception of value. Yet at the same time they are not completely subjective. One can come to an understanding of another's grief from a recollection of grief in one's own life or from a comparison of the reactions of several people suffering grief. Hence the impartial observer recognizes the presence, the reality of grief even though he cannot measure the degree of intensity of subjective feelings. Thus the aforementioned subjective elements enter into the judgment as to the extraordinariness of the means *only* when they have special *objective* relevance.

---

[70] NOLDIN-SCHMITT, *Summa theologiae moralis*, II, p. 307, n. 325: "Quaenam media censeantur extraordinaria communi hominium aestimatione diudicandum est."

[71] The almost unanimous judgment that grave danger was sufficient to constitute the perpetuity of the impediment of impotence was also the judgment that means involving such danger were extraordinary and not obligatory. The fact that so many individual authors came to this conclusion shows that the determination of extraordinariness can be objectively made. See section c) above, pp. 80-81.

7

John Ford illustrates quite clearly what we mean here in an article in *The Linacre Quarterly*.[72] He discusses whether blood transfusions (which are a theoretically ordinary means) can be considered an extraordinary means for a Jehovah's Witness who is firmly convinced that blood transfusions are forbidden by the law of God. His analysis is as follows:

> This raises the question as to how far one may take into account subjective feelings, subjective errors, mistaken attitudes etc. in estimating what is ordinary and extraordinary. At first it might seem strange that subjective errors and attitudes can be the determinants of objective morality. A little reflection will show that it has been customary with moralists to allow subjective elements to be taken into account in making the moral judgement as to what is ordinary or extraordinary in a given case.

He then lists the examples that we have already seen of the Carthusian monk and the modest virgin.

> From all this I would conclude that subjective elements and mistaken subjective attitudes may sometimes be taken into account when deciding the objective obligation to make use of a given procedure.... I see no inconsistency in admitting that this frame of mind (of the Jehovah's Witness) is a *circumstance* which makes the transfusion for him an extraordinary means of preserving life. And it does not seem contradictory to me to admit that while his reason for refusing is objectively mistaken and groundless, nevertheless *his frame of mind* can become at the same time an *objective* excuse from the moral obligation which would otherwise be present.[73] [Author's emphasis]

Ford is not alone in holding this opinion. McFadden agrees with his assessment that a frame of mind can be an objective circumstance which contributes to making a specific means actually extraordinary for the individual.[74]

---

[72] JOHN FORD, "The Refusal of Blood Transfusions by Jehovah's Witnesses," *The Linacre Quarterly*, 22 (1955), 3-10.

[73] *Ibid.*, pp. 5-6.

[74] McFADDEN, *Medical Ethics*, p. 276. Cf. HERVADA, *La impotencia del varon en el derecho matrimonial canonico*, pp. 226-227: "El criterio para distinguir el caracter ordinario o extraordinario de un medio no puede ser subjectivo si con ello nos referimos al conjunto de circunstancias solo privativas del sujeto, pero si cuando con ello queremos indicar las circunstancias del defecto en si."

It is for this reason that the earlier moral theologians admitted what some have called *subjective* elements as constitutive factors in the determination of an extraordinary means.[75] In reality such circumstances are *special objective circumstances relative to the individual*. Hence in these cases one must use the individual rather than the average man as the norm of judgment. The use of the individual norm leads to the conclusion that the means in this case is *actually* extraordinary, though *theoretically* ordinary.

## 7. *Practical Criteria for Determining Extraordinariness*

Now that we have seen the speculative basis for our definition of extraordinary means, only one task remains before returning to the main point of this dissertation, the notion of perpetuity. The authors dealing with medical ethics provide simple, practical criteria for determining whether a means is extraordinary or not: grave inconvenience and reasonable hope of benefit.[76] How do these criteria relate to the notion of extraordinary means that we have presented so far?

It might seem that these are added external factors which must be present in order to declare a means truly extraordinary. In fact, the Rotal decision coram Sabattani of 10 April 1959 speaks about extraordinary means in the context of the perpetuity of impotence and declares that the criterion of extraordinary means is distinct from that of the reasonable hope of benefit.[77]

Kelly, too, had first thought of these elements — inconvenience and usefulness — as separate necessary criteria for

---

[75] JOHN GOODWINE, "The Physician's Duty to Preserve Life by Extraordinary Means,» *Proceedings of the Catholic Theological Society*, 7 (1952), 128.

[76] See GERALD KELLY, *Medico-Moral Problems* (St. Louis, Mo., 1959), pp. 132-133. Here he speaks of two criteria: inconvenience and usefulness. HEALY, *Medical Ethics*, p. 61, speaks of moral impossibility and uselessness as criteria for judging extraordinary means. O'DONNELL, *Morals in Medicine*, p. 70, speaks of uselessness and grave hardship. McFADDEN, *Medical Ethics*, p. 267, speaks of grave hardship or inconvenience and on p. 282 of the reasonable hope of success. JOHN P. KENNY, *Principles of Medical Ethics* (Westminster, Md., 1961), p. 117, mentions grave inconvenience and little hope of success.

[77] c. SABATTANI, 10 April 1959, *ME* 84 (1959), 633, n. 12: «Utrumque criterium debet separatim ab altero examinari. Nec potest unum ab altero absorbi....»

constituting an extraordinary means. Yet, later on in a second article in *Theological Studies* of 1951, he comes to the following conclusion about these criteria:

> It was proposed, however, — and I agree with this — that to avoid complications, it would be well to include the notion of usefulness in the definitions of ordinary and extraordinary means.
> Ordinary means are all medicines, treatments and operations, which offer a reasonable hope of benefit and which can be obtained and used without excessive pain or other incon- venience. [78]

In our opinion, this is undoubtedly the proper way to view these criteria. They are not separate extraneous factors but are the criteria necessary for reason to judge the presence of disproportion which constitutes the means as extraordinary. Hence they are not *separate* conditions or prerequisites, but are the *usual* criteria by which one determines extraordinari- ness.

The *Regulae Iuris* contained two famous axioms: *Nemo te- netur ad impossibile; nemo tenetur ad inutile.* The notion of extraordinary means is the practical result of applying these two axioms to a concrete situation. The criteria developed by the medical ethicians are the results of translating the time- tested axioms into modern terms.

## 8. *Conclusion*

We have found it necessary to make this rather long di- gression from the main theme of discussion, the perpetuity of the impediment of impotence, precisely because of the very close relationship between the concept of perpetuity and that of extraordinary means. The natural complexity of the latter concept does not allow of a simplified presentation if one is really to grasp its full meaning. The history of the concept of extraordinary means has shown this.

The body of classical teaching on the subject of extraordi- nary means provides illustrations which are so antiquated that one finds it difficult to discern the principle behind them.

---

[78] GERALD KELLY, "The Duty to Preserve Life," *Theological Studies*, 12 (1951), p. 550.

Modern texbooks on medical ethics provide so many practical directives to doctors using technical examples that once again one finds it difficult to determine just what it is that makes a means extraordinary. The relativity involved in the concept arising as it does from a multiplicity of ends, circumstances, norms and relationships seems at first to exclude a general notion of extraordinary means. Yet the recognition of the two norms of judgment, the common man and the individual, leading to the distinction between theoretically and actually extraordinary means, allows us to come up with the following definition: A means is extraordinary when right reason judges that there is *inconvenience* in attaining an end by this means *sufficient* to excuse the average man, *or* an individual in special circumstances, from any obligation to use this means. Such a definition coheres with both the classical and modern teaching on the notion of extraordinary means.

The practical criteria used by many moralists are not separate required characteristics but are guidelines by which one can determine *the natural disproportionality* between the use of this means and the attainment of the end *which constitutes extraordinariness*.

Any one of a series of means could be extraordinary insofar as it is a disproportionate means to that end; properly speaking, however, an extraordinary means is one that is gravely disproportionate to the end, in a hypothesis positing an *obligatory* end and *only one* means. This is the situation of moral impossibility.

For purposes of comparison with the idea of perpetuity, it is sufficient to note that both classical and modern scholars sum up all that has been said about extraordinary means in one sentence: An extraordinary means is one that is morally impossible to use in the concrete circumstances. As Tournely concisely put it: means are extraordinary "cum huiusmodi media moraliter impossibilia sint...." [79]

---

[79] TOURNELY, *De universa theologia morali*, III, *de 5° praecepto*, c. 2, concl. 2, s. v. *quartus casus*, p. 425; AERTNYS-DAMEN, *Theologia moralis*, p. 528, n. 566: "...enim talia media habentur improportionata atque moraliter impossibilia."; KELLY, «The Duty of Using Artificial Means of Preserving Life," p. 204: "In other words, an extraordinary means is one which prudent men would consider at least morally impossible with reference to the duty of preserving one's life.»; JOSEPH DONOVAN, *Homiletic and Pastoral Review*, 49 (1949), 904: "When theologians speak of people being excused from prolonging life, if they can only do this

## C. The Concept of Perpetuity Is Equivalent to the Concept of Extraordinary Means

The phrase "moral impossibility" seems to be the key to determining the relationship between the concept of extraordinary means and our notion of the perpetuity of the impediment of impotence. In our discussion above we saw that the concept of perpetuity involved three circumstances or situations. If any one of the three circumstances were present, then the impediment would be perpetual:

1. In a situation in which the physical condition of impotence actually endures until the death of the impotent person, or where removal of the physical condition involves a miracle, or something beyond human powers, the impediment is perpetual.

2. In a situation where removal of the physical condition involves an immoral or illicit act, the impediment is perpetual.

3. In a situation where removal of the physical condition involves danger, the impediment is perpetual.

Hence on page 63 we defined perpetuity as a *quality* of a particular situation seen in relation to the ends of marriage which determines that in such a situation there is a physical or at least a *moral inability* for an average person to assume the rights and obligations to place acts *per se aptos ad prolis generationem.*

In the section immediately preceding this, we saw that extraordinariness was a *quality* of a particular situation seen in relation to an end which determines that in such a situation there is at least a *moral impossibility* for the average person to attain the end by the use of this means. Hence the two concepts seem exactly parallel, equivalent.

---

by extraordinary means, these theologians mean that no one is bound to do the morally impossible any more than he is bound to do the physically impossible."; Healy, *Medical Ethics*, p. 77: "His duty is limited to the employing of means that are morally possible. The means may be physically possible; but if they are not morally possible, one's obligation to use them to preserve life is at an end."; Goodwine, *Proceedings of the Catholic Theological Society*, p. 128; McFadden, *Medical Ethics*, p. 280.

Our object in this section will be to investigate the historical teaching on a perpetuity from the point of view of the relationship between the idea of perpetuity and that of extraordinary means. If we should find that the authors teach that an impediment is perpetual because all the circumstances envisioned involve at least a moral impossibility [80] to attain the ends of marriage, then we could legitimately conclude that the notion of perpetuity equals the notion of extraordinary means. Thus by saying an impediment is perpetual, we would mean either the physical condition of impotency could not be removed at all, or it could only be removed by an extraordinary means.

On page 102 we listed the three circumstances embraced in the concept of perpetuity. They describe the three situations, the three ways in which a physical condition of impotence is judged incompatible with the ends of marriage. The marriage is invalid because of this incompatibility, not because of the presence or absence of the physical condition. In all three situations, the reason for the incompatibility with the ends of marriage is a moral impossibility to fulfill those ends, those purposes. In all three circumstances, then, the impediment of impotence exists precisely because in those circumstances the average person would be *morally unable* to give or assume the right and obligation to place acts *per se aptos ad prolis generationem.*

1. *The Common Doctrine of Canonists and Theologians Holds that All the Circumstances Embraced by the Concept of Perpetuity Involve a Moral Impossibility to Give or Assume the Right and Obligation to Sexual Intercouse*

The teaching of the authors about the first situation of perpetuity is quite clear: when the physical condition of impotence actually perdures until death, there is an evident moral inability to give a right or assume an obligation to sexual intercourse. They teach that a person who will never actually be able to give over the use of a right nor ever actually fulfill an obligation, cannot morally give that right or assume that obli-

---

[80] c. BONET 22 December 1960, 52, p. 607, n. 17: "... quia, ipso naturae iure, contractus materia sive physice sive moraliter possibilis sit oportet."

gation: *nemo potest sese obligare ad impossibile.*[81] The physical impossibility of sexual intercourse prevents one from assuming moral rights and obligations with regard to that action.

### a) Removal of the Physical Condition of Impotence by a Miracle Is so Extraordinary that Such Removal Must Be Considered morally impossible

There can be no question that the authors taught that removal of the impotent condition by a miracle was something both physically and morally impossible for any human being. Removal by a miracle was something beyond the powers of man, supernatural, fortuitous.[82] A miracle was beyond man's powers because it depended on the will of one person, God, and could not be a necessary result of an action of human nature.[83] Hence it was a means of cure both physically and morally impossible for any man to bring about. Laymann tells us quite

---

[81] THOMAS AQUINAS, *Commentarius posterior super libros Sententiarum Petri Lombardi*, dist. 34, q. 1, art. 2, ad 4um: "Ideo talis defectus matrimonium impedit, quia matrimoniium est quaedam obligatio ad carnalem copulam; nullus autem potest ad impossibile se obligare..."; also, *idem, Supplementum Tertiae Partis Summae Theologicae*, q. 58, art. 1, ad 4um; SCOTUS, *Quaestiones in lib. IV Sententiarum*, dist. 34, q. 1, p. 728, n. 2: "Praeterea in contractu isto obligat se ad actum istum, si petatur; sed huiusmodi actus est sibi impossibilis etiam si petatur: ergo obligat se ad impossibile: obligatio ad impossibile est nulla ex lege divina: ..."; SANCHEZ, *Disputationum de sancto matrimonii sacramento*, II, lib. 7, disp. 92, p. 334, n. 2: "Et ratio utriusque partis ea est: quod perpetuae impotentiae repugnet obligatio ad copulam coniugalem ex matrimonio consurgens. Impossibilium enim nulla potest esse obligatio."; SALMANTICENSES, *Cursus theologiae moralis*, II, tract. 9, c. 12, punct. 9, p. 160, n. 107.

[82] SOTO, *In Quartum Sententiarum*, II, dist. 34, q. 1, art. 2, p. 245: "Secus si per miracula: quia natura matrimonii non pendet a miraculo."; CASTRO PALAO, *Opus morale, de virtutibus et vitiis contrariis*, Pars 5ª, tract. 28, disp. 4, punct. 14, p. 161, n. 2.

[83] Cf. SANCHEZ, *Disputationum de sancto matrimonii sacramento*, II, lib. 7, disp. 94, p. 349, n. 11. Here Sanchez has a discussion about the perpetuity of *maleficium* because its removal depended on the will of one, the devil. In *ibid.*, lib. 5, disp. 5, p. 400, n. 5, he discusses the idea that something dependent on the will of one person is impossible. For example, something that can only come about by a dispensation is to be considered impossible because it depends on the will of one lawgiver. "Et confirmatur quia *quod tantum potest fieri per remedium extraordinarium*, ut dispensationem *dicitur impossibile*." (Emphasis mine). The conclusion to be reached from this is: that which is morally impossible is an extraordinary means.

clearly that a removal of the physical condition by a miracle must be considered something morally impossible: "Denique etsi per miraculum tolli possit, nihilominus, moraliter rem aestimando, impossibilis est curatio." [84]

The authors also teach that the other circumstances embraced by the concept of perpetuity also involve a moral impossibility to give or assume the right and obligation to sexual intercourse. But in these circumstances the moral impossibility arises not from the physical impossibility of sexual intercourse, but from the fact that the removal of the physical condition in these circumstances would be so extraordinary, so incongruent, so disproportionate a means that it would be morally impossible.

b) *Removal of the Physical Condition of Impotence by an Illicit or Immoral Act Must Be Considered Something Morally Impossible for All*

Sanchez is once again the spokesman of the common teaching when he explains why it is morally impossible to remove the physical condition of impotence by an illicit or sinful action: "Cum enim id solum dicamur posse, quod licite possumus praestare; impedimentum quod sine peccato auferri minime valet, dicitur impossibile ablatu ac perpetuum." [85]

---

[84] LAYMANN, *Theologia moralis*, lib. 5, tract. 10, pars 4, c. 11, p. 383, n. 1; cf. also Sanchez, *Disputationum de sancto matrimonii sacramento*, II, lib. 7, disp. 93, p. 341, n. 9; PEREZ ab UNANOA, *Opus morale theologicum de sancto matrimonii sacramento*, disp. 37, sect. 1, p. 409, n. 3.

[85] For reference, see previous footnote. To assure the reader that the use of moral impossibility in this sense is legitimate, let him consult pp. 87-89 above. ADALBERTUS VAN DUIN, "De impedimento impotentiae psychicae in iure canonico," *Apollinaris*, 23 (1950), pp. 150-153, discusses the question whether a man is impotent if the only way he can consummate his marriage is by an illicit means. He uses this exact quote from Sanchez to show that impotence must be considered perpetual if a man can be potent only by using immoral means. His conclusion: "In iure enim nostro aequiparantur: licite non posse et simpliciter non posse." See also CAPPELLO, *De matrimonio*, n. 349; HERVADA, *La impotencia del varon en el derecho matrimonial canonico*, p. 227: "La imposibilidad moral de curacion de la impotencia hace a esta juridicamente perpetua."

c) *Removal of the Condition by a Means Involving Danger of Death or Serious Illness Must Be Considered Something Morally Impossible for at Least the Average Person*

The authors give at least two reasons why removal of the condition by a means involving danger would be morally impossible. First of all because it could be illicit to endanger one's life or health to enter a marriage contract since this is not a necessary contract.[86] Furthermore ,it would be morally impossible to expect the average person to undergo such danger in order to fulfill the purposes of marriage.[87] As the Theologians of Salamanca briefly indicate: "... quia durissimum esset aliquam cum tanto imcommodo ad copulam matrimonii obligare." [88]

Thus it is evident that in all the situations embraced by the concept of perpetuity, the removal of the physical condition of impotence involves a moral impossibility. Pontius clearly saw this because he tells us that neither law, prudence nor right reason dictate that such a physical condition be removed, if removal would involve a preternatural, an illicit or a dangerous means. Not only does law, right reason and prudence not dictate the removal of the condition under such circumstances, but law, right reason and prudence positively prevent one from submitting to the removal of the condition under such circumstances.[89]

---

[86] HENRIQUEZ, *Summae theologiae moralis*, lib. 12, c. 7, p. 725, n. 8, nota k: "... quia foemina non intendit cum certo vitae periculo transferre corpus in virum, neque id licere."; c. LEFEBVRE 23 March 1961, *Dec.* 53, p. 151, n. 3.

[87] See opinions of Reiffenstuel, Alphonsus de Liguori, Roncaglia, and Tournely indicated in footnote 25 of this chapter.

[88] SALMANTICENSES, *Cursus theologiae moralis*, II, tract. 9, c. 12, punct. 10, p. 161, n. 116.

[89] Cf. PONTIUS: reference and text given in footnote 24 of this chapter. In the second part of this quote, Pontius is equating the moral impossibility present in the 2nd and 3rd situations of perpetuity with the highest degree of moral impossibility (*impotentia absoluta ordinis spiritualis* - according to Michiels). Our position is that such a degree of moral impossibility is present only in the 2nd situation of perpetuity. VAN DUIN, "De impedimento impotentiae psychicae," pp. 150-154, indicates that impotence is perpetual precisely because of the extraordinariness present in situation 3, and the immorality in situation 2. Sabattani, in the decision of 10 April 1959 (*ME* 84 [1959], p. 623) envisions an operation involving danger as an illicit rather than an extraordinary means. He

Thus in all these circumstances the impediment is perpetual, — there is a moral inability to give over the right and assume the obligation to sexual intercourse — but this moral inability does not arise directly from the physical impossibility for sexual relations but rather from the moral irremovability of the condition because of the extraordinariness involved.

## 2. A Perpetual Impediment Is One that Can Be Removed Only by an Extraordinary Means

Perpetuity exists in all these situations precisely because of this moral inability. The presence or absence of the physical condition is inconsequential; the impediment is perpetual, the marriage invalid, because of this moral impossibility to give or assume a right or obligation to sexual intercourse. Hence it is quite clear that perpetuity is a quality of a particular situation in relation to the ends of marriage which determines that in such a situation there is a moral inability for the average person to attain those ends.

As we saw on page 101, a means is extraordinary precisely because the use of that means in a particular situation would constitute a moral impossibility. Thus the two notions of perpetuity and extraordinary means are equivalent: they both mean the same in the context of the impediment of impotence. Both tell us why the impediment of impotence exists in a particular situation; both tell us why this particular marriage is invalid.

Hence they can be interchanged; we can say: a physical condition that would require an extraordinary means to remove it constitutes the impediment of impotence; or, the impediment of impotence is perpetual when the physical condition of impotency can be removed only by the use of an extraordinary means.

concludes that the impediment would be perpetual in this case because of the illicitness of such a means. Our opinion is that such an operation would be extraordinary because a means involving risk to life is disproportionate to the goal of attaining potency. Hence any operation to cure impotency involving serious danger is *ipso facto* an extraordinary means.

### 3. *A Temporary Impediment Is One that Can Be Removed by Ordinary Means*

If our above conclusion is correct, then its opposite must also be true: the impediment of impotence is temporary if the physical condition can be removed by an ordinary means.

An ordinary means as we have seen above is one that is proportionate to the end to be attained; commonly available; both physically and morally possible for the average person to use in the concrete situation.

In fact, the authors do describe temporary impotence or a temporary impediment in just such terms. Of course, such a description would only have become prevalent after 1600, after perpetuity was recognized as a concept rather than as a fact of the temporal-spatial order.

Frequent expressions used describe a temporary impediment as one that can be removed "per opus humanum," [90] "arte humana," [91] "media ordinata," "medicinae artis, medicamine." [92] All of these expressions clearly indicate that a temporary impediment is one that can be removed by means that are proportionate to the end to be attained, i.e., by natural, ordinary human means such as surgery or medicine which are apt for this purpose.

Furthermore, the authors make a very important distinction when speaking about the removal of an impediment by supernatural means such as that of a miracle. Most were very careful to distinguish the different consequences of cure by a miracle from other types of spiritual (and in a sense superna-

---

[90] Authors who used the expression "per opus humanum": INNOCENT III, X, IV, 15, c. 6; IOANNIS ANDREAE, c. 6, p. 51, n. 29; SOTO, art. 1, p. 238: "humano remedio"; SANCHEZ, p. 341, n. 9; GUTIERREZ, p. 305, n. 21; CASTRO PALAO, p. 161, n. 2; SALMANTICENSES, p. 161, n. 113. (In this and the following footnotes — 91-97 — in order to avoid undue repetition, yet present the results of our research, we will cite only the author, plus the specific pertinent reference. Full information may be obtained by comparing with bibliography).

[91] The following authors used the expression "arte humana": DE CONINCK, p. 812, n. 76; BARBOSA, p. 561, n. 3; TOURNELY, II, c. 14, p. 746: "artis remedia"; PICHLER, p. 504.

[92] SALMANTICENSES, p. 160, n. 105: "nullo medicamine, nulloque arte"; FERRARIS, p. 203: "artis medicae"; WERNZ-VIDAL-AGUIRRE, p. 263, n. 221: "per ordinaria medicae artis subsidia"; CAPPELLO, p. 332, n. 346: "ordinaria artis medicae subsidia"; CONTE A CORONATA, p. 387, n. 306: "ordinaria artis medicae remedia."

tural) cures brought about by prayer, penance or the rites of exorcism. The reason for the distinction was that a miracle is an unusual, unaccustomed, unavailable, undependable way of removing the impediment.[93] In short, it was extraordinary. On the other hand, prayer, penance, conversion, or the exorcisms of the Church were usual, customary, commonly available means for the removal of the problem.[94] Thus removal by prayer, penance or exorcism meant that the impediment was temporary because it was removed by ordinary means.

Finally the authors described a temporary impediment as one that could be removed by natural [95] and licit means.[96] Thus a temporary impediment is one that can be removed by ordinary, natural means that are physically and morally possible for the average person to use. Laymann quite explicitly identifies a temporary impediment as one that can be removed by an ordinary means: "Nam hoc ipso apparebit impotentiam fuisse tantum temporalem, *seu ordinario medio curabilem, . . .*" [97]

---

[93] BONACINA, I, q. 3, pt. 13, p. 297, n. 4: "modo extraordinario et insueto"; BARBOSA, p. 561, n. 3: "modo extraordinario et insueto"; SALMATICENSES, p. 163, n. 131: "insueto modo"; WERNZ-VIDAL-AGUIRRE, p. 292, n. 233.

[94] SOTO, art. 3, p. 250; SANCHEZ, p. 341, n. 8; DE CONINCK, p. 812, n. 76; "ordinariis," p. 813, n. 85: "soleat"; BONACINA, p. 297, n. 4: "modo consueto"; LAYMANN, p. 383, n. 1: "Verum sanatio per consuetos Ecclesiae exorcismos, licet supernaturalis sit, non tamen in hoc eventu miraculosa reputatur, quando quidem veluti ordinarie provenit."; BARBOSA, p. 561, n. 3: "modo consueto"; REIFFENSTUEL, p. 114, n. 5; SALMANTICENSES, p. 160, n. 105; SCHMIER, p. 113, n. 61: "consuetis et ordinariis."

[95] SANCHEZ, p. 349, n. 10; GUTIERREZ, p. 305, n. 21; REIFFENSTUEL, p. 114; SCHMIER, p. 107, n. 80; ERNRICUS PIRHING, *Ius canonicum*, IV: *De sponsalibus et matrimonio* (Dilingae, 1678), lib. 4, tit. 15, p. 142, n. 1, p. 144, n. 11; SCHMALZGRUEBER, p. 152, n. 3; PICHLER, p. 504, n. 3; RONCAGLIA, p. 202; ROSSET, II, p. 558, n. 1379; AERTNYS-DAMEN, p. 635, n. 710; GASPARRI, p. 331, n. 542.

[96] Most of the same authors in the same places.

[97] LAYMANN, p. 383, n. 2. See also, PEREZ ab UNANOA, p. 414, n. 3; PONTIUS, c. 61, p. 442, n. 3; SCHMALZGRUEBER, p. 198, n. 100: ". . . quippe cum perpetua impotentia dicatur omnis illa, quae per ordinaria et licita media non potest tolli. . . ."

4. *Conclusion*: Perpetuity is a concept determining a quality of a particular situation of impotence which specifies why that situation is incompatible with the ends of marriage. This quality consists in a moral inability to attain the ends of marriage arising from either the physical inability to engage in sexual intercourse or from the moral impossibility of removing the physical condition of impotence.

In Chapter One we investigated the origin of the requirement of the perpetuity of impotence. In chapters two and three our purpose was to investigate the meaning of perpetuity through a historical study of the phrase "impedimentum perpetuum" used by Innocent III.

A quick glance at the literature sufficed to show that there were two seemingly contradictory interpretations of the meaning of "impedimentum perpetuum." The first held that an impediment is only perpetual if it actually perdures until the death of the impotent person. Any cure, any removal of the impediment will indicate beyond doubt that such an impediment was only temporary. Such is the common teaching of the early canonists such as Innocent IV, Hostiensis, Ioannis Andreae and Panormitanus.

Yet later canonists and theologians such as Laymann, Sanchez, Castro Palao, Reiffenstuel, Schmalzgrueber and the Theologians of Salamanca clearly teach that the presence or absence of the physical condition of impotence is not the important factor in determining the perpetuity of the impediment. They treat perpetuity as a concept, rather than a fact; they define circumstances and situations in which the impediment is perpetual, even though the physical condition of impotence has in fact been removed.

What, then, is the real meaning of perpetuity? How can these contrary positions be harmonized? Is perpetuity a fact or a legal concept?

The first step leading to an answer to the above questions is a recognition of the true meaning of the impediment of impotence itself. Even today many people confuse the *impediment* with the physical condition of impotence. This confusion was also quite evident throughout the history of the treatment of this subject.

Controversies over the possibility of relative impotence constituting the impediment led to an important distinction

around the year 1600. From that time on the notion of impediment began to be distinguished from the physical condition of
impotence which had been identified with the term impediment, giving it a very physiological connotation. Due to this
distinction, the impediment of impotence no longer needed to
be exclusively identified with a natural biological condition; it
could be recognized as something more: a principle of the
juridic order. From identification with the physical inability
to engage in sexual intercourse, the impediment now began to
be seen as it really was: an incompatibility with the ends of
marriage.

This broader fuller understanding of impediment accordingly led to a fuller meaning of its modifier "perpetual." Perpetual always meant, and still means: enduring in time, last-
ing until the death of the impotent party. But this is not its
exclusive, nor its primary meaning in the context of the impediment of impotence. Used in conjunction with "impediment"
understood as a relation of incompatibility with the ends of
marriage, "perpetual" came to signify a quality, a characteristic of a particular situation of impotence which determined
that a moral inability to give over the right and assume the
obligation to sexual intercourse was present.

Thus "perpetual" now primarily refers to the concept of
perpetuity, a concept which specifies the reason why a particular situation of impotence is incompatible with the ends of
marriage.

The concept of perpetuity embraces three circumstances,
three situations of impotence:

1. The situation in which the physical condition of impotence actually endures until the death of the impotent person,
or where it can only be removed by a miracle, or some means
beyond human powers.

2. The situation where the physical condition can only be
removed by an immoral or illicit act.

3. The situation where the physical condition can only be
removed by a means involving danger of death or serious illness.

In all of these circumstances, the impediment of impotence is said to be perpetual because the physical condition is
judged incompatible with the ends of marriage. Thus there is

no real contradiction between the factual and the conceptual interpretations because the concept includes situation 1, the situation of fact. Perpetuity, then, is a legal concept indicating a quality or characteristic of the above situations which specifies why those situations invalidate a marriage.

What, then, is this quality, this characteristic? Chapter Three is an attempt at an answer to this question. Here we investigated in detail the situations mentioned by the authors seeking to determine what the common quality, the common characteristic of each situation was.

Common to each of the situations embraced by the concept of perpetuity was a moral impossibility to assume an obligation to sexual intercourse. In the first situation, the physical impossibility of sexual intercourse itself gave rise to the moral inability to assume an obligation. In the other two situations, the moral impossibility arises from the fact that the physical condition can only be removed by an extraordinary means.

Yet an extraordinary means is itself something which makes it morally impossible for an average man to attain an end by the use of such a means. Extraordinariness is the quality of a situation which determines that it is morally impossible for the average person to attain the end by the use of this means. Thus the concept of perpetuity and the notion of extraordinary means seem to be equivalent. Both indicate a characteristic of a particular situation which makes it morally impossible to attain a particular goal or end.

In conclusion, then, a perpetual impediment is one in which the physical condition cannot be removed at all, or can only be removed by the use of an extraordinary means. A temporary impediment is one in which the physical condition can be removed by the use of ordinary means.

CHAPTER FOUR

# THE PERPETUITY OF THE IMPEDIMENT OF IMPOTENCE IN THE WRITINGS OF MODERN AUTHORS AND IN ROTAL JURISPRUDENCE

C. 1068 of the Code of Canon Law promulgated by Pope Benedict XV in 1917 did not depart in any way from the traditional teaching of canonists on the impediment of impotence. The purpose of the Code was not to create new law but to codify existing law; hence Innocent III's requirement of perpetuity has juridical force in existing Church law because of its inclusion in C. 1068, No. 1:

> Impotence, antecedent and perpetual, whether on the part of the man or the woman, whether known to the other party or not, whether absolute or relative, invalidates marriage by the law of nature itself.

## A. CONTINUITY WITH EARLIER TEACHING ON PERPETUITY

The Code defines neither perpetual impotence nor the requirement of perpetuity; however, the official annotations citing C. 33, c. 1, 2 and 4 as well as X, IV, 15, c. 1-3, 5-7 together with the rule provided by C. 6, No. 2 of the Code leave no doubt that perpetuity must be understood according to the common doctrine of the approved authors whose teaching we have just investigated.[1]

Accordingly, one of the characteristics of the teaching of modern authors and modern Rotal jurisprudence on perpetuity will be a basic continuity and identity with previous teaching. The Code, however, did clarify certain aspects of impotence which had been the source of diverging opinions among the

---

[1] C. 6, No. 2: "Canones qui ius vetus ex integro referunt, ex veteris iuris auctoritate, atque ideo ex receptis apud probatos auctores interpretationibus, sunt aestimandi."

earlier authors.  Thus it specifies that a physical defect of the female can constitute the impediment just as well as a physical defect of the male.  Furthermore, it gives special emphasis and recognition to relative impotence as a true constituent of the impediment.  Finally, the Code definitely rejects the opinion of Peter Lombard and Thomas Aquinas that impotence, if known and accepted by the potent party, does not nullify.[2] Hence there is no theoretical dispute about these points among the authors of the modern period.

Because of this basic continuity with earlier centuries, we can expect to find elements in the writings of modern authors favoring both the factual and conceptual understanding of perpetuity.

1. *Elements in the Literature and Jurisprudence of the Modern Period* (1900 *to the Present*) *Which Indicate a Predominantly Factual Understanding of Perpetuity*

One might well ask: How is it possible for the factual understanding of perpetuity to persist into the modern period if earlier authors taught that perpetuity was a juridic concept? Would not this earlier teaching have the effect of making later authors abandon a predominantly factual understanding of perpetuity?

The persistence of the factual understanding of perpetuity can be accounted for when one realizes that earlier authors had only *implicitly* taught that perpetuity was a juridic concept.  It is quite true that by the time of Sanchez the understanding of perpetuity had advanced to a point where one *could* logically deduce that perpetuity must be a concept and not a mere factual event.  But such a possibility is not the same as a clear, unequivocal, explicit teaching that perpetuity is a juridic concept.  Such a clear, explicit teaching about perpetuity as a concept and about its relation to the idea of extraordinary means was only to develop in the Rotal jurisprudence of the past twenty years.

Another reason for the predominance of the factual understanding of perpetuity is the quite natural tendency to equate

---

[2] For an understanding of the position of Peter Lombard and Thomas Aquinas on this point, see pages 25-28 of Chapter One as well as footnotes 37 and 38 of that chapter.

the impediment of impotence with the organic condition which gives rise to it. Even the Code speaks of perpetual impotence as nullifying a marriage. Yet such phraseology can be misleading because impotence, *as a biological condition*, whether perpetual or temporary, whether antecedent or subsequent, has no relevance *per se* on the validity or invalidity of the marriage. Canonically, the impediment of impotence is not the inability to have sexual intercourse, but rather the inability to give over the right and assume the obligation to place acts *per se aptos ad prolis generationem*.[3] Thus it is only when an organic or functional condition of the genital apparatus prevents one from assuming the rights and obligations to perfect copula that the impediment of impotence exists and nullifies the marriage. The writers of the modern period were no more immune from the natural tendency to equate the impediment of impotence with the condition of impotence than were the authors of earlier periods.

A third reason for the persistence of the factual understanding of perpetuity was the cultural milieu, *Weltanschauung*, or mind-set of the authors of this period caused by changed circumstances.

Classical authors such as Sanchez, Laymann and Pontius were able to accept the reality of the *impediment* of impotence even when no organic cause for the physical inability to have sexual intercourse could be ascertained. They could explain such a situation by attributing the cause to the invisible influence of the devil working through a *maleficium*. Furthermore they had a practical method of proving the existence of such an impediment, the special canonical institute known as the *experimentum triennale*.[4] Thus a solution to these cases was possible on the local level by an ecclesiastical annulment for relative impotence.

By the year 1900, however, a change of mentality had taken place regarding the granting of annulments in general, and specifically in regard to the problem of relative impotence. The Church felt called not only to safeguard the indissolubility of marriage as she had traditionally done, but also to *militantly*

---

[3] See c. STAFFA 12 October 1951, *Dec.* 43, p. 626, n. 2. Also, KEATING, *Bearing of Mental Impairment*, p. 180; Finnegan, "The Current Jurisprudence," p. 443.

[4] For more information about this *experimentum triennale*, see D'AVACK, *Cause*, pp. 526-531; also SANCHEZ, *Disputationum de sancto matrimonii sacramento*, II, lib. 7, disp. 107, pp. 381-383.

defend Christian marriage against even the appearance of favoring dissolubility. The theoretical battle for indissolubility against Protestant theologians and absolutist as well as atheistic statesman led to practical reforms which, in reality, severely limited the real possibility of granting annulments.

Insofar as relative impotence was concerned, the tendency to abandon supernatural explanations for natural ones — together with a growth in confidence in the experiential and natural sciences — led to a rejection of the possibility of impotence *ex maleficio*. Yet the sciences of psychology and psychiatry had not yet been developed. Thus the authors of the late 1800's and the early 1900's had no ready explanation for cases of functional impotence, i.e. a situation in which a couple could not consummate their marriage even though no organic cause for the dysfunction could be ascertained.

Their solution to such problems was to seek the papal dispensation for a *ratum et non-consummatum* marriage. The *experimentum triennale* had fallen into desuetude probably as a result of the centralization of Church structures after the Council of Trent and the certainty offered by the papal dispensation.[5] This seemed to be a much better method of solving such cases because a uniform practice could be established for the whole Church; the difficult problem of proof of relative impotence could be avoided as well as the possibility of having to rescind a judgment of nullity if it should turn out that the impediment were not perpetual.

The cumulative effect of all these developments was to dissuade the authors from any further explicitation of perpetuity as a juridic concept. For the granting of an annulment on the basis of a perpetual impediment of impotence, when the physical condition of impotence no longer exists, appears to favor the dissolubility of marriages. Furthermore, the question could readily be solved by a papal dispensation. Hence we find elements that point to a predominance of the factual understanding of the perpetuity of the impediment of impotence among modern authors. Only in the 1950's does the pendulum swing to a conceptual understanding of perpetuity. This development is

---

[5] For information about the disappearance of the canonical institute of the *experimentum triennale*, see WERNZ-VIDAL-AGUIRRE, *Ius matrimoniale*, p. 273, n. 223; CONTE A CORONATA, *De matrimonio*, p. 373, n. 299, and p. 383, n. 306; GASPARRI, *De matrimonio*, p. 332, n. 542.

largely due to the pioneering efforts of judges of the Sacred
Roman Rota.

### a) *Identification of the Impediment of Impotence with an Organic Cause*

The authors of the modern period show the same tendency
as the early canonists to equate the perpetuity of the impediment
of impotence with the incurability of the organic cause of the
physical condition of impotence. Wernz significantly quotes a
24 January 1871 decision of the Sacred Congregation of the
Council:

> At nostra aetate antequam propter impotentiam coëundi ex
> frigiditate vel caliditate nullitas matrimonii declaretur, sedulo
> inquirendum est, num revera illius impotentiae coëundi adsit
> causa perpetua et incurabilis. [6]

Genicot reflects the same mentality; [7] even Cappello seems
to equate perpetual impotence with a defect of the genital
organs:

> Impotentia, quae dicitur oriri e maleficio, numquam est per-
> petua, quia numquam *de facto* secumfert laesionem in organis
> corporis. Eatenus enim admittenda est generatim ut perpetua,
> quatenus aliquis defectus in organis existat. [8]

Following this line of thought, the Rota equates perpetuity
with incurability.[9] A decision c. Pinna goes so far as to say that
the Rota's policy of not admitting functional impotence (i.e.
cases in which an organic cause cannot be ascertained) as truly
constituting the impediment of impotence is a *wise one*. Such
a policy is wise because functional impotence is based on causes

---

[6] F. X. WERNZ, *Ius decretalium*, IV$^2$: *Ius matrimoniale* (Prati, $^2$1912),
p. 147, nota 33.

[7] GENICOT, *Theologiae moralis Institutiones*, II, p. 559, n. 504: "Igitur,
cum hodie satis constet impotentia *fere semper e defectu naturali oriri,*
censenda erit perpetua tantum quando arte medica vel operatione
chirurgica nullatenus aut nonnisi cum discrimine vitae tolli potest."
(Emphasis mine).

[8] CAPPELLO, *De matrimonio*, p. 347, n. 365.

[9] c. MANNUCCI 28 January 1935, *Dec.* 27, p. 42: "...ideoque impedimentum habetur si ille rerum status certo demonstretur antecedens matrimonium, perseverans in matrimonium et *omnino insanabilis...*" (Emphasis mine); c. QUATTROCOLO 14 February 1941, *Dec.* 33, p. 3, n. 5.

which are not perpetual of their very nature.[10]  In general, the
reasoning in this decision presents the same view of perpetuity
as a duration of a factual condition in time as Innocent IV or
Hostiensis held.[11]

A definite change from this preoccupation with the perpetuity of the cause of the impotence is found in a decision c. Fiore
20 December 1963.  Here it is clearly indicated that the impediment is constituted not by the perpetuity of the organic or med-
dical cause of the physical condition but by the perpetuity of
the inability to have intercourse, regardless of the cause from
which it arises.[12]  Such a situation will be more difficult to prove
because it is not based on medical evidence, but we have no
reason to deny its theoretical possibility.

A decision c. Staffa 12 October 1951 provided the basis for
this new approach by recalling that the impediment of impotence, rather than being a mere physical inability for sexual
intercourse, is more correctly a moral inability to give over the
right and obligation to sexual intercourse.[13]  Finally, a decision
c. Sabattani 9 October 1964 points out quite clearly that the
juridical notion of perpetuity is not equivalent to the *peritus'*
determination of the perpetuity of a biological defect.  The judge
is the one who must consider and determine whether a particular
defect constitutes the impediment and whether its perpetuity
or curability is adapted to the juridic order.[14]

---

[10] c. PINNA 4 July 1959, *Dec.* 51, p. 352, n. 4: "*Sapienter* proinde
constans iurisprudentia Ordinis Nostri vix, immo ne vix quidem, habuit
impotentiam functionalem tamquam impedimentum dirimens matrimonium, utpote dubiae perpetuitatis."

[11] *Ibid*: "Difficilior adhuc evadit probatio perpetuitatis, quoties de
vitio mere functionali agitur, cum influere soleant *causae quae de natura
sua non sunt perpetuae*: aliquando enim decursu temporis praeter ex-
pectationem remittunt vel per curationem cessant." (Emphasis mine).

[12] c. FIORE 20 December 1963, *Dec.* 55, p. 991, n. 3: "Ad effectum irri-
tandi nuptias absolute seu abstracte *nihil confert origo idest causa in-
ducens* incapacitatem sive in viro sive in muliere ponendi actus coniugales: ideo et doctrina et iurisprudentia canonica impedimentum impotentiae agnoscunt *iure merito* ubi illud provenit ex nervorum morbos,
sed etiam ubi causis dumtaxat psychologicis adscribendum est; unde
et de psychica impotentia, tamquam de functionali impotentia specie,
sermo est." (Emphasis mine).

[13] c. STAFFA 12 October 1951, *Dec.* 43, p. 626, n. 2.

[14] c. SABATTANI 9 October 1964, *Dec.* 56, p. 694, n. 12.

b) *Practical Refusal to Admit Relative Impotence as Perpetual and as Constituting the Impediment*

In theory, all the post-Code authors admit the possibility of relative impotence as truly constituting the impediment. The explicit provisions of C. 1068, No. 1, as well as the history of the impediment of impotence require such an admission. A great many modern authors pay lip service to this principle, but then immediately warn that such a principle can have no practical effect.[15] Wernz-Vidal-Aguirre note that Sanchez wisely admits relative impotence as truly constituting a form of the impediment, but then warn the reader that such a form of impotence should not easily be admitted in practice. Their assertion that relative impotence can often be cured by medical means is just another way of stating the opinion that relative or functional impotence cannot be perpetual because it is not based on an organic cause.[16]

In an attempt to reflect an enlightened approach to the question of diabolical influence, the authors of the modern period dismiss relative impotence but fail to provide any practical relief within the context of the impediment of impotence for those cases of impotence based on an indiscernible cause. The only solution they propose is to have the parties seek a papal dispensation for a *ratum et non consummatum* marriage.[17]

The same attitude is quite evident in many Rotal decisions. In a decision c. Parrillo 24 April 1933, the court reacts to an argument for a declaration of nullity on the basis of relative impotence for a modern day *mulier arcta* by quoting Innocent

---

[15] IOANNIS CHELODI, *Ius matrimoniale iuxta codicem iuris canonici* (Tridenti, ³1921), p. 74, n. 73: "Praesertim hodie haud ita facile impotentia viri mere functionalis, in foro, ut perpetua admittitur." He says relative impotence is possible, and then adds: "Hanc sufficere *theoretice*, ex natura rei, explorati iuris est; *practice* raro esse perpetuam, quia per medicam artem curari potest..." (Emphasis mine); CAPPELLO, *De matrimonio*, p. 333, n. 346: "In praxi non facile admittenda est impotentia relativa tamquam perpetua, quia saepius per artem medicam facile curari potest."

[16] WERNZ-VIDAL-AGUIRRE, *Ius matrimoniale*, p. 265, nota 16: "...at in praxi non facile admittenda est impotentia relativa tamquam perpetua, eo quod saepe per artem medicam curari possit."

[17] WERNZ, *Ius decretalium*, IV², p. 152, n. 347: "Quare si peracto experimento copulae per triennium nulla consummatio sequatur, per se sententia pro nullitate matrimonii ex impotentia absoluta vel relativa potest ferri, vel potius omisso triennali experimento peti dispensationem matrimonii rati."; also, D'AVACK, *Cause*, pp. 564-566.

III's phrases: "impedimentum illud non erat perpetuum" and "cognoscibilis erat illi cuius simili commiscetur". Notwithstanding the Code's approval of relative impotence, the court rejects a first instance decision for nullity because of the situation of impotence arising from a woman with a tough hymen being united with a weak husband. This court prefers to follow Aquinas's opinion that there can be no masculine perpetual impediment regarding one woman and not all others, rather than follow the provisions of the Code.[18]

Hence the Rota seemed to have made a practical determination that it would not concern itself with deciding cases of relative impotence. It seemed to have adopted quite seriously Innocent IV's adage: "Melius videtur quod propter maleficium [or relative impotence] nullum matrimonium separandum sit", notwithstanding C. 1068, No. 1. In cases of functional impotence we read the almost ritual reply that such a type of impotence cannot be perpetual or at least cannot be proven to be perpetual. Invariably, the solution suggested is to seek the papal dispensation.[19]

Only after the important decision of Sabattani of 10 April 1959 do we find a new willingness to seriously investigate the perpetuity of functional and relative impotence.

### c) *Appeal to Future Events as a Determinant of the Perpetuity of the Impediment*

A final element indicating a predominantly factual understanding of perpetuity is the need to see perpetuity as conditioned by future facts. Innocent III reflected this view when he pointed out so long ago: "De talibus enim non sit facile iudicandum, quum finale iudicium pendeat ex futuro".

If perpetuity is seen primarily as a fact of duration in time, then the future will be a decisive factor in determining perpetuity and with it the validity or invalidity of the marriage.

Certain decisions of the Rota seem to uphold this view.

---

[18] c. PARRILLO 24 April 1933, *Dec.* 25, pp. 258-259, n. 3; p. 261, n. 8. The reference to Thomas Aquinas is *Supplementum Tertiae Partis Summae Theologiae*, q. 58, art. 1, ad 5um.

[19] For a list of Rotal decisions which refuse to treat the perpetuity of functional impotence and instead suggest the dispensation, see D'AVACK, *Cause*, p. 565, nota 2. See also Sabattani's remarks about this practice in the decisions 22 June 1952 *IDE* 64 (1953-II), p. 370, and 10 April 1959 *ME* 84 (1959), pp. 621-623.

The court c. Parrillo 24 April 1933 held that a judge had to have moral certitude about the future perpetuity of the impotence in order to be able to grant a decision of nullity.[20] Two decisions c. Jullien reflect the same opinion.[21]

Following this principle, the court c. Morano on 18 April 1931 reached the controversial decision that a previously given annulment must be revoked because the man had in fact regained potency (understood here as the ability to emit true semen through unoccluded spermatic ducts) as the unexpected side result of an operation on his genital organs. The argumentation was based on the fact that the future had proved that his impediment was not perpetual.[22]

A similar decision c. Quattrocolo 3 January 1940 declares that a woman who was supposed to be too *arcta* in relation to her husband could not now have a perpetual impediment because she would certainly now be apt with regard to her husband due to the effects of pregnancy and childbirth arising from an adulterous relationship with another man.[23] Thus future facts determine the perpetuity of the impediment.

Such a position is, in reality, quite untenable. The dependence of perpetuity and with it of the validity or invalidity of the marriage on future events cannot be reconciled with the sanctity and indissolubility of marriage. As long ago as the time of the Glossators, writers had seen that perpetuity could not really be dependent on the future. Antonius a Butrio reports

---

[20] c. PARRILLO 24 April 1933, *Dec.* 25, p. 258, n. 2: "Non sufficit igitur certitudo impotentiae in actu, sed certum quoque esse oportet illam fuisse antecedentem et futuram perpetuam, ut iudex coniugii nullitatem decernere possit. Certitudo haec, quoad *perpetuitatem futuram,* haberi solet liquida cum agitur de impotentia organica...." (Emphasis mine).

[21] c. JULLIEN 16 February 1940, *Dec.* 32, p. 144: "Non raro igitur iudicium prudens *pendet ex futuro*; in praesenti autem, impotentia, saltem quoad eius perpetuitatem, solummodo probabilis videtur..." (Emphasis mine); c. JULLIEN 16 April 1943, *Dec.* 35, p. 302: "...ratio atque iurisprudentia docent vitia functionalia tamquam perpetua haud expedite habenda. *Prudens enim iudicium ex futuro saepe pendet...*" (Emphasis mine).

[22] c. MORANO 18 April 1931, *Dec.* 23, p. 134, n. 7. This controversial decision gave rise to much serious discussion among the authors. See A. C. JEMOLO, *Il matrimonio nel diritto canonico* (Milano, 1941), p. 111 in footnote; P. D'AVACK, "L'impotenza generativa maschile nel diritto matrimoniale canonico," *IDE* (1951-I), p. 402; VITALE, «La perpetuità dell'impotenza," p. 61.

[23] c. QUATTROCOLO 3 January 1940, *Dec.* 32, n. 16.

the objection to Innocent III's comment about the decision resting with the future: "... quia matrimonium non potest esse in pendenti".[24] He responds that the marriage itself is not hanging in the balance, it is only our knowledge about it and our declaration of its validity or invalidity which depends on the future.[25]

It is only with the decision c. Sabattani 10 April 1959 that Rotal jurisprudence began to address itself to this problem. Only by understanding perpetuity as a juridic concept rather than a situation of fact can we truly resolve what seems to be a dependence of the validity of marriage on the merely contingent. Sabattani points out that the validity of the contract cannot depend on medical progress; there must be a definite moment in which the medical perpetuity of impotence is determined and this moment can only be the time of the contract.[26] Thus there is no such thing as future perpetuity, Parrillo notwithstanding.[27] The appeal to what the future may bring can have no effect on determining the perpetuity of the impediment, nor the validity of the marriage because the perpetuity of the impediment of impotence is a juridic concept not a mere factual event. This is now the common Rotal opinion.[28]

---

[24] ANTONIUS A BUTRIO, *In libros decretalium commentarii*, VI, lib. IV, tit. 15, c. 6, p. 41, n. 33.

[25] *Ibid.*: "Matrimonium non potest esse in pendenti quo ad veritatem et substantiam vinculi, quia vel statim est vel non est, sed bene certificatio et declaratio an sit, quo ad nostri cognitionem, et sic potest esse in pendenti."

[26] c. SABATTANI 10 April 1959, *ME* 84 (1959), p. 634, n. 13: "Nam validitas contractus non potest esse incertitudini obnoxia, et dependens a continuo fluxu artis medicamentariae.... Statui ideo debet determinatum omnino tempus, relate ad quod iudicetur de possibilitate vel minus medendi impotentiae: et hoc esse non potest nisi tempus matrimonii."

[27] c. SABATTANI 22 February 1963, *ME* 89 (1964), p. 167: "Evidens enim est quod tempore celebrationis elementa validitatis contractus adesse debent, inter quae recensetur materia possibilis.... Ideo dici potest quod, iuxta speciem iuris, non existit nec praecedens nec futura conditio obiectiva diversa, sed tantum illa quae in coniugibus praesens est tempore contractus."; VICTOR DE REINA, "Impotencia y esterilidad," *Ius Populi Dei* (Miscellanea in honorem Raymundi Bidagor), III (Romae, 1972), 461.

[28] c. SABATTANI 10 April 1959, *ME* 84 (1959), p. 633, n. 13: «... possibilitas medendi, quae postea apparuerit, quaeque antea non fuerit specifice praevisa, nullo modo relevat. Neque relevat progressus scientiae medicae, generice praevisus."; c. BONET 22 December 1960, *Dec.* 52, p. 606, n. 10: "Perpetuitas... ex tunc iudicari debet, idest tempore celebrati matrimonii.... Itaque impotentia quae dum nuptiae ineunt insanabilis in-

## 2. Persistence of the Full Definition of Perpetuity, Containing the Implicit Recognition of Perpetuity as a Juridic Concept in the Modern Period

As we indicated earlier, the modern period did not substantially alter the teaching on perpetuity which had been developed by the classical authors.[29] Thus, though the factual understanding of perpetuity predominated, the conceptual interpretation was never totally overlooked because it persisted in the many definitions of perpetuity given by the principal authors. These authors discuss the three situations of perpetuity, and most are careful to use a specific term for each situation, thereby showing that perpetuity must include all of these situations. Furthermore these definitions implicitly teach that perpetuity is a juridic concept and that it is related to the notion of extraordinary means.[30] The persistence of the conceptual understanding of perpetuity is best attested to by the specific contribution of the modern period which will now be described.

---

dubie sit, perpetua dicenda est. At eidem medendi possibilitas, quae postea supervenit, quaeque antea specifice praevisa non fuit, nullius est momenti."; c. SABATTANI 20 March 1964, *Dec.* 56, p. 253, n. 4: "...possibilitas harum operationum remedialium conspici debet relate ad tempus nuptiarum, non vero ad tempus processus. Id evidenter statui debet in linea iuris."; c. LEFEVBRE 4 December 1971 (unpublished decision, Protocol Number 9478, 227/71.): "...perpetuitas impotentiae, uti conceptus iuridicus et non merus eventus facti attenditur tempore ipso contractus.... Proinde attendendum est utrum necne perpetuitas accurate probetur isto tempore celebrationis matrimonii, independenter quidem ab aliis circumstantiis, quae possint addi solummodo posterius...."

[29] HARRINGTON, "The Impediment of Impotency," p. 208.

[30] That perpetuity is implicitly recognized as a juridic concept and that it is related to extraordinary means can be gleaned from a comparison of the following references from authors of the modern period. CAPPELLO, *De matrimonio*, p. 332, n. 346; CONTE A CORONATA, *De matrimonio*, p. 387, n. 306; JEMOLO, *Il matrimonio nel diritto canonico*, p. 109; B. MERKELBACH, *Summa theologiae moralis*, III: *De Sacramentis* (Brugis, [10]1956), p. 887, n. 876; HERVADA, *La impotencia del varon en el derecho matrimonial canonico*, p. 223. For Rotal jurisprudence, see c. SEBASTIANELLI 17 February 1917, *Dec.* 9, p. 32, n. 2, and p. 36, n. 8; c. JULLIEN 16 February 1940, *Dec.* 32, p. 142, n. 3.

B. THE SPECIFIC CONTRIBUTION OF THE MODERN PERIOD TO THE
PERPETUITY OF THE IMPEDIMENT OF IMPOTENCE

Throughout our discussion of the understanding of perpetuity in the modern period, we noticed at first a strong predominance of the factual understanding of perpetuity and then a
later change of emphasis to the conceptual understanding. This
leads to the question: what new insights or developments can be
singled out as the specific contribution of this period to the
understanding of the concept of perpetuity?

1. *Authors of the Modern Period "Explicitly" Recognize Perpetuity as a Juridic Concept Rather Than a Fact of Duration
   in Time*

Perpetuity was implicitly recognized as a juridic concept in
the writings of many canonists and moral theologians who from
1600 onwards attributed more importance to the circumstances
and conditions of the removal of the physical condition of impotence than to the actual presence or absence of that physical
condition.[31] The specific contribution of the modern period has
been to explicitly, clearly, and unequivocally teach that the
perpetuity of impotence is a juridic concept, not a mere situation
of fact.[32]

2. *Authors of the Modern Period "Explicitly" Recognize the
   Relationship of the Concept of Perpetuity with the Notion
   of Extraordinary Means*

Earlier writers had implicitly related the concept of perpetuity with the notion of extraordinary means by recognizing
that a perpetual impediment of impotence was present in a
situation in which one would have to use a miracle an immoral
means or a means involving danger in order to remove a physical
condition of impotency, precisely because such means were seen

---

[31] See footnote 23 of Chapter Three.
[32] c. SABATTANI 10 April 1959, *ME* 84 (1959), p. 620, n. 5; c. BONET 22
December 1960, *Dec.* 52, p. 608, n. 21; c. SABATTANI 22 February 1963,
*ME* 89 (1964), p. 161; c. SABATTANI 20 March 1964, *Dec.* 56, p. 253; c. SABAT-
TANI 9 October 1964, *Dec.* 56, p. 694, n. 12; c. POMPEDDA 10 June 1970,
*ME* 96 (1971), p. 205, n. 5; c. LEFEBVRE 3 December 1971, P.N. 9478, 227/71.

as extraordinary, disproportionate to the end and non-obligatory. In such situations, these authors recognized that a marriage was invalid because the average person could not be expected to give or assume the right and obligation to perfect copula under such conditions. Hence the extraordinariness of these circumstances creates the same moral inability to give or assume the obligation as does the perpetual physical impossibility of sexual intercourse.

The specific contribution of the scholarship of these past few decades has been to make the above implicit connection of perpetuity with the notion of extraordinary means quite explicit.

The explicitation of this relationship is largely the result of the judicial sentences c. Sabattani, one of 22 June 1952 issued when he was a judge of the Regional Tribunal of Bologna, and others of 10 April 1959, 22 February 1963 and 9 October 1964 issued when he was Auditor of the Sacred Roman Rota.[33]

What was the process by which Sabattani came to make this explicit connection between perpetuity and the idea of extraordinary means? As we have already seen in pages 80-81 of Chapter Three, the third situation of perpetuity, — the situation involving danger — is the natural communicating link between these two concepts. Reflection on the reason why the dangerousness of an operation would be sufficient to nullify a marriage, leads one to ponder whether the moral principles concerning ordinary and extraordinary means could have any influence on determining the perpetuity of the impediment of impotence. Others had seen this implicit connection earlier,[34] but Sabattani in the important decision defining perpetuity of 10 April 1959 has the merit of logically illustrating the relationship of the third situation of perpetuity with the notion of extraordinary means.

This important case dealt with a man whose blocked spermatic ducts rendered him canonically impotent. The question before the court was: Is this man perpetually impotent? It would seem not, since an operation involving no danger to life or health

---

[33] The decision of 22 June 1952 is published in *IDE* 64 (1953-II), 367-377. See the preceding footnotes for references to these other decisions of Sabattani.

[34] See pages 102-107. Also CAPPELLO, *De matrimonio*, p. 332, n. 346; CONTE A CORONATA, *De matrimonio*, p. 387, n. 306; D'AVACK, *Cause*, p. 554; HERVADA, *La impotencia del varon en el derecho matrimonial canonico*, p. 224.

was possible. The condition could be overcome; therefore the impediment would not be perpetual.

In seeking a solution, the court first reminds us that perpetuity is a juridic concept not a situation of fact. Accordingly juridical reasons are of more weight and consequence in determining perpetuity — which is of the order of rights and obligations — than factual situations such as a successful or unsuccessful operation. The distinction between a perpetual and a temporary impediment must be based on something more than surgical skill.

What is this difference? Why does removal of the physical condition in some circumstances constitute the impediment as temporary, while the same removal in other circumstances constitutes the impediment as perpetual? Various authors had given contradictory explanations; the one constant principle, however, seemed to be that if the removal of the physical condition of impotence involved bodily danger, then the impediment would be perpetual.

In the decision of the Regional Tribunal of Bologna of 22 June 1952, Sabattani had posed the question: Why does danger of death make the impediment perpetual? One answer would be that the grave inconvenience of submitting oneself to danger would free one from any obligation to remove the physical condition causing the impotence. But if such a principle should be admitted, one would logically have to ask why do not the authors use this criterion of grave difficulty as the criterion of perpetuity rather than restricting the criterion of perpetuity to the gravest of all difficulties, the danger to life itself? Sabattani is unable to provide an answer and leaves the question open.[35]

In this decision of 10 April 1959 he attempts to provide an answer by stating: danger is the criterion of perpetuity because only danger is an illicit means; grave inconvenience does not suffice because it would still be licit to remove the physical condition in those circumstances.[36]

The concentration of attention on an operation as a dangerous means logically leads to two criteria by which one would

---

[35] c. SABATTANI 22 June 1952, *IDE* 64 (1953-II), 371: "Ast [*sic*] si admittitur principium 'gravis incommodi', non intelligitur quomodo debeat postea applicatio restringi ad incommodum illud gravissimum, quod est discrimen vitae."

[36] c. SABATTANI 10 April 1959, *ME* 84 (1959), p. 623, n. 6, compared with p. 626, n. 9.

judge whether any obligation to undergo an operation for the removal of the physical condition of impotence existed. If the operation would be an extraordinary means, one would not be obliged to make use of it. Therefore, the impediment of impotence would be perpetual. If the operation offered no reasonable hope of success, one would likewise not be obliged to make use of it and the impediment would be perpetual.

By this process of reasoning, Sabattani is led to develop the two criteria by which one may judge the perpetuity of the impediment of impotence: the operation must not be an extraordinary means and it must offer a reasonable hope of success.

The means can be extraordinary not only by reason of the danger involved, but also because of the complexity of the operation and the skill required. A reasonable hope of success is required because no one can be obliged to undergo such inconvenience for a vain attempt. There must be a reasonable proportion between what the person is enduring and the good that he hopes to attain.[37]

Thus a modern writer for the first time demonstrated the explicit connection between the concept of perpetuity and the notion of extraordinary means. The close relationship between these two concepts has become a recognized principle of Rotal jurisprudence.[38]

### 3. Authors of the Modern Period "Explicitly" Recognize the Notion of Perpetuity as a "Relative" Notion

The modern period has made another very important contribution to the concept of perpetuity; it has recognized that perpetuity is a relative notion. A decision c. Pompedda 10 June

---

[37] Ibid., p. 625: "Non potest enim quis adigi ad subeundam notabilem iacturam suorum bonorum, turbari a sua condicione habituali, ac compelli ad subeunda discrimina diuturnae curationis et chirurgicae incisiones longe a sua domo, ut tantum corpus suum praestet ad experimentum, cuius exitus incertus praevidetur.

Ut obligatio oriri possit, necesse est ut bona, quibus, arripiendo operationem, valedicit, compensentur cum certa spe aliorum bonorum aequalis saltem valoris, quamvis alterius generis."

[38] c. PINNA 2 March 1958, Dec. 50, p. 201, n. 2; c. SABATTANI 22 February 1963, ME 89 (1964), p. 161; c. SABATTANI 20 March 1964, Dec. 56, p. 253, n. 4; c. LEFEBVRE 4 July 1964 Dec. 56, p. 554, n. 15; c. DI FELICE 28 November 1968, ME 94 (1969), 102; c. POMPEDDA 10 June 1970, ME 96 (1971), p. 207, n. 6, and p. 209, n. 8.

1970 could scarcely be more explicit with regard to this point: it states that the perpetuity of the impediment of impotence is a relative notion because one must judge the possibility or probability of recovering potency by taking into consideration the time, place and individual circumstances of the persons involved.[39]

The decision c. Pompedda is not an isolated one; in fact, as far back as 15 November 1909, the Rota in a decision c. Persiani declared a woman to have a perpetual impediment of impotence simply because she was unable to have a simple hymenectomy due to the fact that she lived in an underdeveloped country where no doctors were available. Cappello, Wernz-Vidal-Aguirre, Conte a Coronata all seem to agree with this decision because they quote it in their manuals.[40]

But does not this lead to an absurdity? Must we not conclude that the validity or invalidity of marriage depends on the presence or absence of a doctor? If such a principle be accepted, one would also have to accept its logical conclusions. Thus a doctor might be available, but his fee might be very high. A rich woman could afford to retain him, but a poor woman could not. Therefore the validity or invalidity of marriage would, in the last analysis, depend on the amount of money one has!

A decision c. Mattioli 25 July 1956 even goes so far as to take into consideration a person's subjective fear of an operation as a circumstance contributing to the perpetuity of his impotent condition.[41]

---

[39] *Ibid.*, p. 205: "Quo igitur questio enodetur de perpetuitatis notione, statim ac imprimis asserendum est eam esse notionem relativam, idest conferandam esse cum locis, cum personis, cum remediis in regione exstantibus, cum tempore, in quibus casus singuli versantur atque probabilitatem vel possibilitatem obtinent recuperandae sanitatis."

[40] c. PERSIANI 15 November 1909, *Dec.* 1, p. 140, n. 13; CAPPELLO, *De matrimonio*, p. 333, n. 346: "Possibilitas moraliter aestimari debet, scilicet omnibus circumstantiis sive locorum sive personarum consideratis. Hinc non repugnet quod in una regione, ubi desunt auxilia artis medicae, impotentia relativa ut perpetua habeatur, dum in alia regione aestimatur temporanea ob artis medicae auxilium."; CONTE a CORONATA, *De matrimonio*, p. 388, n. 306; WERNZ-VIDAL-AGUIRRE, *Ius matrimoniale*, p. 263, nota 13.

[41] c. MATTIOLI 25 July 1956, *Dec.* 48, p. 737, n. 2: "Nec praetermittendum est horrorem ac diffidentiam erga chirurgi actionem esse quid omnino personale ac diversum in singulis hominibus. Sunt qui multum valent et multa agerunt in bello, in quibuslibet periculis spernendis et aggrediendis et superandis, vel in vehiculis aëriis, inter difficultates maximas, dirigendis, etc. quique tamen ita trepidant coram medici dentarii

Does not this make perpetuity ultimately dependent on the will of the impotent person? How can this relativity be reconciled with the teachings of the earlier authors? The Theologians of Salamanca had explicitly stated: "... perpetuitas impotentiae dirimens, non ex voluntate, sed *ex natura rei* dependet..."[42] (Emphasis mine). Schmalzgrueber writes in the same vein: "... impedimenti perpetuitas non pendet ex voluntate patientis impedimenti, neque ex eo, quod tollatur, vel non tollatur, sed ex eo, quod, *spectata rei natura*, tolli, vel non tolli possit absque vitae periculo".[43] (Emphasis mine)

The answer to all these objections, in our opinion, is to recognize that perpetuity is a relative notion, but that it is not purely relative.

The term *relative* implies a relation. When we say that perpetuity is relative, we must ask: relative to what? One might respond: perpetuity is relative to the future — to future events which might restore potency, to future developments of medical science which might cure a person's present condition. Yet the fact that perpetuity is a juridic concept shows that it cannot be completely dependent on contingent future events. As Sabattani has pointed out in a decision of 22 February 1963, and as Antonius a Butrio noted long ago — the elements of validity (the object of the contract of marriage) must be present at the time of marriage either in *re* or in *spe*, that is with the sure knowledge that they will be present at sometime in the future.[44]

Perpetuity, then, is relative to objective circumstances present at the time of the marriage. Such is the common teaching of the authors, especially in the modern period.[45]

---

instrumentis et actibus, ut vix resistere ac tolerare valeant, et viribus aliquando deficiant, talia simpliciter aspicientes."

[42] For the reference, see footnote 23 of Chapter Three.

[43] SCHMALZGRUEBER, *Ius ecclesiasticum universum*, IX, tom. IV, part 3, tit. 15, p. 173, n. 44.

[44] See footnotes 25-28 of this chapter.

[45] See footnotes 39-41 of this chapter. See also c. FELICI 10 July 1959, *Dec.* 51, p. 378, n. 6; c. BONET 22 December 1960, *Dec.* 52, p. 607, n. 17; "In definito casu... ratio habenda est circumstantium re existentium in contrahentibus." and n. 13: «Criterion raritatis deducendam est e peculiaribus circumstantibus personarum matrimonium contrahentium."; c. LEFEBVRE 23 March 1961, *Dec.* 53, p. 151, n. 2: "Praetermittendum non est recursum ad media sanationis apta quandoque pendere a locorum temporumve circumstantiis..."; c. SERRANO 22 October 1971, P.N. 10,321 187/71, nn. 13-32: "Potissima consideratione dignum in iudi-

The earliest indication of this relativity, this dependence on objective circumstances, that our research has been able to discover is contained in a commentary by an Irish Franciscan, Antonius Hiquaeus, on *Quaestiones in lib. IV Sententiarum* of John Duns Scotus. In discussing perpetuity, Hiquaeus raises the question: Would impotence be perpetual if the medical treatment needed to cure it were difficult to obtain or very costly? He replies without hesitation that in such a case the circumstances render the impediment perpetual.

How is this possible? Hiquaeus proceeds to explain. In such circumstances, the impediment is not in the power of the spouses, either in themselves or through others; consequently just as in the case of *maleficium*, the impotence is here and now perpetual with regard to these two people; thus they are incapable of attaining either the use or the ends of marriage.[46]

Hiquaeus's comparison of this situation to that of relative impotence due to *maleficium* brings to mind Sanchez's explanation of the basic reason why relative impotence nullifies: the actual circumstances and conditions in which a particular couple find themselves make it impossible for them to hand over the right and obligation to sexual intercourse.[47]  Furthermore, such an impossibility does not have to result from a condition which would affect everyone (e.g. absolute impotence based on an organic cause) but can result from a true impossibility which only affects these two persons in relation to one another. This relative impossibility certainly is sufficient to nullify the marriage, because marriage is not an abstract reality; it either exists

---

cio canonico nobis visum est agere de charactere 'relativo' penes impotentiam functionalem."

[46] Antonius Hiquaeus' treatment of this subject is found in Scotus, *Opera Omnia*, IX: *Quaestiones in lib. IV Sententiarum*, ed. cura Fr. Minorum Hibernorum Regularis Observantiae Collegii S. Isidori Romae cum commentario Antonii Hiquaei (Lugduni, 1639), dist. 34, q. 1, p. 743, n. 15: "Respondetur simpliciter in eo casu, et *circumstantiis reddi impedimentum perpetuum* et aequivalere maleficio, quod praesumitur perpetuum, quia sic impedimentum non est in potestate coniugum per se, aut alios, *ac proinde redditur hic et nunc perpetuum respective ad ipsos*, quo sunt inhabiles ad matrimonii usum et finem." (Emphasis mine).

[47] SANCHEZ, *Disputationum de sancto matrimonii sacramento*, II, lib. 7, disp. 94, p. 348, n. 8:  "Si enim impotentia illa perpetua sit, *non potest persona illa* maleficiata *tradere potestatem* sui corporis, *obligando se* ad actum coniugalem, utpote ratione maleficii perpetui est sibi impossibilis. Quare *eadem ratio militat, ac* quando *ratione frigiditatis* vel ciuiuscumque accidentis impotens est." (Emphasis mine).

or does not exist between two concrete particular persons.[48] Hence a situation of impotence is perpetual and nullifies the marriage whenever the circumstances make it impossible for the common generality of mankind, *or for the particular individuals involved in a definite marital situation*, to hand over the right and assume the obligation to perfect copula.

The circumstances causing this impossibility must be objective. Impossibility to hand over a right and assume an obligation must be based on objective considerations, not on the willingness or unwillingness to hand over the right. Impossibility to hand over a right means that that which is to be handed over is not within the effective dominion of the person contracting to hand it over.

It can sometimes happen, though rarely, that internal emotions such as fear, horror, and pain become objective because they are so vehement, so irrational, so strong that they are no longer under the effective dominion of the person involved; hence they must be considered on a par with objective circumstances. Thus a decision c. Mattioli 25 July 1956 describes personal horror and fear in almost objective terms: persons who have been war heroes can be so affected by irrational fear of ordinary medical or dental treatment that they can scarcely tolerate or resist the fear; the mere sight of a dentist's chair is enough to make them faint.[49] In such cases, this type of fear is not dependent on the subjective will of the individual, but must be taken into account as an objective circumstance.

Sabattani also points out that *vaginismus*, even though not dependent on an organic cause but simply arising from the woman's phantasms and imagination, is an objective defect of

---

[48] *Ibid.*, disp. 93, pp. 339-340, n. 3: "Tertio, quia sic se habet absolutum et totale impedimentum respectu matrimonii absoluti, sicut respectivum et particulare, respectu particularis. *Sicut* ergo *illud dirimit omnem matrimonii* contractum, *ita hoc dirimet peculiarem.* Quarto, quia *matrimonium respicit individuam personam,* et *cum illa debet iniri.* Si ergo respectu illius inveniretur impotentia undequaque consurgens, cui nullatenus ope aliqua medicinae subveniri posset, *respectu illius dirimet matrimonium,* non autem respectu aliarum, si cum aliis non esset ea impotentia. *Quia* respectu illius privatae personae *non posset esse obligatio ad copulam,* utpote quae respectu illius est impossibilis: *at potest esse obligatio cum aliis,* cum quibus est possibilis. (Emphasis mine)

[49] See footnote 41 of this chapter.

the genital organs and must not be considered as dependent on the person's will.[50]

In short, perpetuity is a relative notion, but it is not completely relative. Perpetuity is not completely relative because it will *always* be a quality of a situation of impotence producing the inability to give or assume the right and obligation to perfect copula. It will be relative insofar as the objective circumstances of any situation of impotence can vary. It will also be relative because a true concept of perpetuity can be determined on the basis of the norm of the average person in those circumstances, and an equally true and valid concept of perpetuity can be based on the norm of the individual couple in their actual existential situation.[51]

The ancient dispute over the refusal to recognize relative impotence based on *maleficium* and the refusal of the modern Rota to handle cases of purely functional impotence can really be reduced to a hesitancy to accept the individual couple as a valid norm for the concept of the perpetuity of the impediment of impotence.

As is quite natural, one dealing with a problem in the abstract, uses an abstract norm — the norm of the average man — to establish the principles of his teaching. Thus the classical canonists whom we have studied in Chapter Three gave a definition of perpetuity based on this abstract norm. Such a definition is true and valid; yet perpetuity was equally validly determined in individual cases by Rotal decisions such as the one c. Persiani of 15 November 1909. The Rota deals with concrete individual cases, hence the norm it used to decide perpetuity was the concrete particular situation of impotence. This decision of 1909 establishing the actual perpetuity of the impediment in this case, far from being in contradiction to theoretical perpetuity (viz. that perpetuity arrived at on the basis of the norm of the average man), rather shows that the general or theoretical notion of perpetuity is valid in this par-

---

[50] c. SABATTANI 9 October 1964, Dec. 56, n. 3, plus the reference to *Dec.* 43, p. 452, n. 2.

[51] See Hervada's posing of this question in, *La impotencia del varón en el derecho matrimonial canónico*, p. 224: "En otras palabras, debe estarse al caso general o al concreto? La doctrina canónica ha sequido en este punto un criterio de objetividad relativa al sostener que para calificar de ordinario o extraordinario a un medio había que atenerse a las condiciones ambientales del sujeto."

ticular case because any situation of impotence is truly an impediment to marriage whenever it makes it impossible for either an average couple, *or for this particular couple*, to exchange the rights and obligations to sexual intercourse.

Recent Rotal jurisprudence clearly shows that any hesitancy to accept the individual couple as the norm of perpetuity has been overcome. As a decision c. Bonet 22 December 1960 clearly states: the validity of marriage stands or falls on the objective existence or not, of the object of the matrimonial contract, i.e. the right and obligation to true conjugal acts.[52] Thus the object of the matrimonial contract has to be both physically and morally possible. Such physical-moral possibility has to be decided in a definite case by taking into consideration the real circumstances of the contractants.[53]

The same opinion is held by Anné. If we consider that the lack of the material object of marriage is a lack of consent, then the important observations of Anné in a decision of 16 February 1971 can be applied to our question:

> At vero, cum liberum contrahentis arbitrium consensus matrimonialis sit praecipuus auctor, in unaquaque casu nullitatis matrimonii ob defectus consensus vere matrimonialis, iudices satagant oportet ut quam plenissimae intelligant mentem et voluntatem quibuscumque contrahens ad nuptias accesserit, seu considerent consensum a contrahente praestatum *in existentia sua singulari*, i.e. prout elicitus *erat a tali persona talibusque in rerum adiunctis*.... Nam ipse consensus, *relate ad ipsum contrahentem, est quaedam electio existentialis, cuius contentum haud independens est ab ipsis circumstantiis* in quibus nupturiens statuit se matrimonium cum tali persona initurum esse. [54]

---

[52] C. BONET 22 Decembre 1960, *Dec.* 52, p. 606, n. 13: "Validitas namque, quae in hac circumscripta provincia uno naturae iure regitur, stat vel cadit cum obiectiva existentia vel minus materiae seu causae contractus matrimonialis; idest cum iure tradito et accepto ad actus vere coniugales."

[53] *Ibid.*, p. 607, n. 17: "... quia, ipso naturae iure contractus materia sive physice sive moraliter possibilis sit oportet. In definito casu, ad determinandum num haec physica-moralisque possibilitas revera adsit, iuxta natura iuris, positivis seclusis legibus irritantibus vel inhabilitantibus, ratio habenda est circumstantium re existentium in contrahentibus."

[54] c. ANNÉ 16 February 1971, P.N. 9557 33/71. (Emphasis mine).

Another decision c. Anné 25 February 1969 likewise informs us that judges deciding the invalidity of a particular marriage on the basis of the lack of the formal object of marriage must necessarily base their decision on the existential situation. General principles often do not suffice for the particular case because they are based only on a plurality of cases and do not take all the circumstances into consideration.[55]


## C. Conclusion

### 1. Resumé

The object of Chapter Four has been to study the perpetuity of the impediment of impotence as found in the writings of the authors of the modern period (from 1900 to the present) and in Rotal jurisprudence.

This study has shown the basic continuity of the teaching of this period with the traditional doctrine of earlier eras. Perpetuity is recognized as a situation of fact, but not exclusively so; the recent explicit recognition in jurisprudence that perpetuity is a juridic concept is more than sufficient to counter a tendency at the early part of this period to see perpetuity exclusively as a situation of fact. The result of this whole process of reflection on the meaning of perpetuity in the modern period can be summed up in a phrase of a decision c. Bonet of 22 December 1960: "Unde magis magisque consequitur, perpetuitatem impotentiae esse notionem iuris non merum eventum facti." [56]

The specific contribution of the teaching of this period was threefold: 1) the explicit recognition of perpetuity as a juridic concept; 2) the explicit linking of the notion of perpetuity with the notion of extraordinary means; and 3) the explicit recognition that perpetuity is a relative concept.

---

[55] c. Anné 25 February 1969, *ME* 96 (1971), p. 31, n. 18: "Tandem iudices quorum est definire utrum necne, ex defectu obiecti formalis, constet de invaliditate matrimonii sub iudicio, necessario ponuntur in campo existentiali." and p. 32: "...propositiones ...ad explicandas proprietates essentiales institutorum quae sunt iuris naturalis — prout ratiocinando ab ipsarum rerum existentia coliguntur — saepe sunt vix adaequatae, quia redactae sunt secundum ea 'quae ut in pluribus accidunt, quorum cognitio sufficit ad prudentiam'..."

[56] c. Bonet 22 December 1960, *Dec.* 52, p. 608, n. 21.

## 2. Observations

In our opinion, the explicit connection that Sabattani makes between perpetuity and extraordinary means in the decision 10 April 1959 does not go far enough because he limits this connection to only one situation of perpetuity, the third situation, i.e. one involving an extraordinary medical treatment. He considers extraordinariness only in regard to an operation, and fails to point out that a supernatural or an illicit means of removing the physical condition is equally as much an extraordinary means as a complex operation.   Basically, the concept of perpetuity is related to the notion of extraordinary means because the same reason, a disproportion sufficient to free one from any obligation to remove the physical condition, is present in all the situations of perpetuity.   Each situation of perpetuity, i.e. when removal of the physical condition can only be brought about by a miracle, an illicit means or a dangerous means, posits the extraordinariness of the means of removal; it is precisely this extraordinariness which causes the impotence to be a perpetual impediment.   The extraordinariness of the means of removal causes a physical/moral impossibility of giving or assuming the right and obligation to sexual intercourse.   Hence it is not logically necessary to define a perpetual impediment of impotence as Cappello does by listing the situations of perpetuity, although it might be useful for the sake of clarity.[57]   One could just as accurately, and more briefly, state: the perpetual impediment of impotence exists in a situation in which the physical condition of impotence can only be removed by an extraordinary means.[58]   Of course, it would have

---

[57] CAPPELLO, De matrimonio, p. 322, n. 346:   Quare perpetua est, quando tolli nequit sine miraculo, vel medio illicito vel sine probabili vitae periculo aut sine gravi damno salutis; temporanea quando cessat lapsu temporis, e.g. in impuberibus, vel mediis licitis et sine probabili vitae periculo e.g. per operationem chirurgicam seu ordinaria artis medicae subsidia, quavis cum gravi incommodo, vel per media spiritualia absque miraculo." (Emphasis mine). See also CONTE a CORONATA, De matrimonio, p. 387, n. 306.

[58] LAWRENCE WRENN, Annulments (Hartford, ²1972), p. 8, first lists all the situations of perpetuity but then finds a briefer and clearer way to define "permanent impotence": "Or to put it in another way, impotence is permanent when it is irremediable except by extraordinary means."   A decision c. DI FELICE 28 November 1968, ME 94 (1969), p. 102, given by the Tribunal of Benevento, tells us that the only question one must ask in seeking to determine whether a bodily defect can be

to be made quite clear that the term extraordinary means was
not limited to medical procedures but would include any truly
extraordinary means of removing the physical condition, such
as supernatural or illicit means.

Furthermore, it would be better not to establish separate
positive and negative criteria for perpetuity as the decision
c. Sabattani 10 April 1959 does.[59]  The only criterion should be:
Does right reason judge the means necessary for the removal
of the physical condition to be ordered, proportionate and
congruent to the high value of marriage and to the individual
circumstances of the persons involved so that such a removal
would be both physically and morally possible for those
persons?

Of course, definite practical criteria are necessary so that
one can make such a judgment, but these practical criteria are
not separate, independent requirements; instead, they are elements by which one comes to form the judgment of the extraordinariness of the means of removal; this judgment of
extraordinariness is at the same time the determination of
perpetuity.  Criteria such as those mentioned by the medical
ethicians (grave inconvenience, reasonable hope of success,
usefulness) are all elements which are used to discern if a
means is extraordinary; it is for this reason that they enter
into the judgment of perpetuity.  But to establish only two
criteria, as Sabattani does, is to limit the elements one may
ponder to decide perpetuity.  Furthermore, he treats extraordinary means on a par with the criterion—reasonable hope
of success.  In our view, the criterion of reasonable hope of
success is not a separate, equal, independent criterion of perpetuity, but merely a constituent criterion of the judgment as
to the extraordinariness of the means.

Finally, we would like to point out that the realization that
it would not be right to oblige an individual to use a specific
means to remove the physical condition is a very helpful clue
to ascertaining the presence of the perpetual impediment of

---

corrected is: whether or not it can be cured by an ordinary means:
"Nec alia ratio adhibenda est in conamine sanationis defectus corporis,
ex quo oritur impotentia."

[59] c. SABATTANI 10 April 1959, *ME* 84 (1959), p. 633, n. 12: "Duo tradita
criteria debent simul exigi, ut apte diiudicari possit de perpetuitate impotentiae.... Utrumque criterium debet separatim ab altero examinari.
Nec potest unum ab alio absorbi...."

impotence.  For as we have seen throughout the latter part of this chapter, perpetuity is equivalent to the notion of extraordinary means.  The special characteristic of extraordinary means, however, is that one cannot be obliged to use it, though he may if he so desires.[60]  Hence the judgment that one cannot be obliged to use this specific means of removal of the physical condition, even though it is the only means of removal, is often also the judgment of perpetuity.

With regard to the modern period's recognition of perpetuity as a relative notion, we note that such an explicit recognition strengthens the thesis that perpetuity is equivalent to the notion of extraordinary means.  In our discussion of extraordinary means, we analyzed the relativity of that notion.  In this fourth Chapter the discussion of the relativity of the notion of perpetuity brought out the striking parallelism between the two relative notions.  Such a parallelism confirms the conviction that they are equivalent notions.[61]

Probably the most important contribution of the modern period was precisely the recognition of perpetuity as relative.  Thorough research of the literature of earlier periods has brought to light only one author, Antonius Hiquaeus, who explicitly treats of the relativity of perpetuity.  The implicit identification of perpetuity and extraordinary means evident in the later writers of the period 1600-1900 was most probably the starting point for reflection on this relative characteristic of perpetuity that becomes more prominent in the writings of the modern period and in Rotal jurisprudence.  Rotal decisions, which of their very nature are concerned with the individual case, were, as should be expected, in the forefront of establishing this relative aspect of perpetuity.[62]

The relativity of perpetuity should make us aware that the perpetuity of the impediment of impotence is not a univocal term.  A physical condition of impotence can give rise to a

---

[60] See above, pages 86-87.  Also, PIERO FRATTIN, "Impotence in Canon Law," *The Catholic Lawyer*, 9 (1963), 115: "The extraordinary nature of the means of cure relieve the impotent party of the obligation of restoring his sexual capacity.... It follows as a consequence that, if the only available treatment for a condition of impotence is represented by an operation which may be classified as extraordinary, no moral obligation to undergo it is established and therefore the patient is considered by the law as perpetually impotent."

[61] Compare pp. 90-95 with pp. 127-134.

[62] See references given in footnote 45 of this chapter.

perpetual impediment in a certain situation for a certain individual, while an exactly similar physical condition will only
be a temporary impediment for another individual.   This is
not arbitrary nor contradictory.   It is simply a fact that perpetuity can legitimately and validly be defined using either
the norm of the average man or the norm of the individual.[63]
Generally, the use of either norm applied to a definite physical
condition will result in a uniform judgment of perpetuity.
It can happen, however, that certain special individual circumstances must be taken into account, such as irrational fear,
extreme modesty, extreme poverty, which are not present in
the average case.   In these circumstances one must be careful
to base the judgment as to perpetuity on the individual norm
rather than the norm of the average person.   One is trying to
determine the existence of a perpetual impediment to *this*
marriage, not to marriage in the abstract.   Hence this particular
couple in their existential situation must be the norm.[64]   The
possibility of using either norm for the judgment of perpetuity
does not make perpetuity a purely subjective notion because
there is a constant, an absolute in every case: the situation of
impotence is judged perpetual precisely because it is physi-
cally/morally impossible for the parties in the situation to
give or assume the right and obligation to acts *per se aptos
ad prolis generationem.*

## 3. *Corollary*

Important consequences flow from the fact that perpetuity
is a relative notion equivalent to the idea of extraordinary

---

[63] See FRATTIN, "Impotence in Canon Law," p. 117: " Should, therefore, a patient need this kind of treatment, and should he find himself
in the moral impossibility of profiting from the services of a competent physician, no obligation to seek a cure to his condition would be
imposed.   Such a doctrine would also apply in the case of a very
wealthy person, who could easily approach a skillful surgeon even in
other countries or continents.   Notwithstanding his financial means, he
would not be required to resort to such extraordinary experiments.
Consequently his condition of impotence would be looked upon as perpetual in the mind of the law."

[64] c. SERRANO 22 October 1971, P.N. 10,321 187/71. Here the Ponens
tells us that one must judge a "matrimonium existentiale."   While it
is true that impotence is a concept of possibilities, still "...aliud enim
est mera possibilitas, aliud abstracta possibilitas a realitate aliena."

means.  It is not our task here to investigate what these might be.  Reflection on the following adjustments to the classical canonical definitions of perpetual and temporary impotence should help the reader to form some conclusions of his own:

> Perpetual impotence is that which can be remedied only by extraordinary means.
> Temporary impotence is that which can be remedied by ordinary means.

Another formulation of the same idea would perhaps be even more exact: A condition of impotence which can only be remedied by extraordinary means is canonically perpetual. A condition of impotence which can be remedied by ordinary means is canonically temporary.

One logical corollary is that common, minor, easily remediable defects of the genital organs—such as phimosis (a constriction of the foreskin which prevents the full erection of the male organ or at least its penetration into the vagina) or an impenetrable hymen—can be cured by ordinary means. They cannot, therefore, normally be said to constitute a true impediment to marriage.

However, since perpetuity is a relative concept, these same defects in certain rare circumstances would have to be judged perpetual because in those circumstances the only remedy for the condition would be an extraordinary means.  Thus, if even the simple medical assistance needed to cure such minor defects were lacking in the area where the individual lived, or if he were so destitute as not to be able to afford even this simple cure, the means of remedying the condition would be *actually* extraordinary for him; *as a consequence, the impediment would be perpetual, his marriage invalid.*

Subjective attitudes which are capable of objective evaluation — such as irrational fear of a non-dangerous operation, religious faith, exaggerated modesty — *could also render actually extraordinary for a certain individual means which would be ordinary for the average person.*  Hence such attitudes could be a factor in constituting a condition of impotence canonically perpetual; accordingly they may sometimes have to be taken into consideration in a judgment as to the validity of a marriage.

# CONCLUDING REMARKS

The purpose of this dissertation has been to investigate the origin and meaning of the requirement of perpetuity contained in C. 1068, No. 1. The pursuit of this topic has led us through all the periods of ecclesiastical law from the *Decree of Gratian* to the unpublished decisions of the Sacred Roman Rota. Our findings can be summarized as follows:

1) The "requirement of perpetuity" arose only after general agreement had been reached that the indissolubility of the marriage bond was fixed at the time of the exchange of consent of the parties. Such a theory is a necessary prerequisite for the notion of diriment impediment. In turn, the notion of the diriment impediment of impotence is necessary before one can speak of the "requirement" of the perpetuity of the impediment of impotence.

The requirement of perpetuity became part of the positive matrimonial law of the Church when the Decretal Letter (*Fraternitatis tuae*) of Innocent III to the Bishop of Auxerre was included in the *Compilatio III antiqua* and authentically promulgated by the bull *Devotioni vestrae* in the year 1210.

2) After the adoption of the consent theory it became possible to distinguish the essential *ius in corpus* necessary for marriage, from the simple use or non-use of that right. The requirement of perpetuity was introduced to be a clear and almost absolutely certain sign that the marriage right could not have been handed over at the time of consent; for *nemo dat quod non habet* and *nemo potest sese obligare ad impossibile.*

3) The perpetuity of the impediment of impotence must be understood as a true juridic concept rather than as a situation of fact.

It can therefore be defined as: the quality of a particular situation of impotence which specifies and determines precisely why there is a moral inability to assume the rights and obligations to place acts *per se aptos ad prolis generationem.*

4) Historically, the impediment of impotence has been described as perpetual in three circumstances:

a) When the impotent condition can only be remedied by something beyond human powers such as a miracle.

b) When the impotent condition can only be remedied by some sinful or illicit means.

c) When the impotent condition can only be remedied by a means involving danger or serious bodily harm.

5) An extraordinary means is one which right reason, after careful consideration of the value of the end and of the concrete circumstances, judges disproportionate to the end to be attained; consequently, no one can be required to use it to attain that end. An extraordinary means, properly speaking, gives rise to a situation of moral impossibility.

Several authors of the classical period (1600-1900) saw that the situations constituting a perpetual impediment of impotence involved moral impossibility. They implicitly saw the link connecting these two notions.

It is our contention that perpetuity and extraordinary means are equivalent notions, not only in the third situation of perpetuity (c) above, but in all the situations.

6) One may, therefore, use the following clear, simple affirmation: canonically, perpetual impotence is that which can be remedied only by extraordinary means; temporary impotence is that which can be remedied by ordinary means.

7) Perpetuity is a relative notion. The perpetuity of the impediment must be determined by taking into consideration variant objective circumstances; sometimes subjective circumstances that have objective relevance may also enter into the judgment of the perpetuity of the impediment.

The special contribution of the modern period has been to explicitly demonstrate that perpetuity is a juridic concept and that it is a relative concept.

8) The problem of the application of the requirement of perpetuity does not consist principally in determining the curability or incurability of the physical or other cause giving rise to the impediment; the purpose of the requirement of perpetuity is to indicate, to point out, that an impediment does exist and is *actually verified in this particular case.* One way of doing this, the way required by C. 1068, No. 1, is by determining whether the cause of a physical condition of impotence may be removed or not by ordinary means.

Perpetuity is a requirement of the natural law insofar as the natural law requires some criterion, some means by which a morally certain judgment might be formed that the marital rights and obligations *could not* have been (or simply *were not*) exchanged.

# BIBLIOGRAPHY *

## A. Sources

*Acta Apostolicae Sedis, Commentarium Officiale.* Romae, 1909-1929; post 1929 in Civitate Vaticana.

BERNARDUS PAPIENSIS. *Bernardi Papiensis, Summa decretalium.* Ed. E. Laspeyres. Ratisbonae: apud G. Josephum Manz, 1860.

BURCHARDUS WORMATIENSIS. *Decretorum Libri XX,* in *Patrologia latina.* Ed. J.-P. Migne. Vol. 140. Parisiis, 1853.

*Codex Iuri Canonici Pii X Maximi iussu digestus Benedicti Papae XV auctoritate promulgatus.* Typis Polyglottis Vaticanis, 1948.

*Corpus Iuris Canonici.* Ed. Aemilius Friedberg. Vol. I: *Decretum Magistri Gratiani.* Vol. II: *Decretalium Collectiones.* Lipsiae, ²1879 [photo-offset edition: Graz, 1955].

*Corpus Iuris Civilis.* Vol. I: *Institutiones, Digesta.* Ed. P. Krueger. Vol. II: *Codex Iustinianus.* Ed. P. Krueger. Vol. III: *Novellae Constitutiones.* Ed. G. Kroll. Berolini: apud Weidmannos, 1954.

GRATIANUS. *Decretum divi Gratiani totius propemodum iuris, cum in textum, tum in Glossis ...geminae lectioni ...omnia restitutae.* Lugduni: apud Hugnonum a Porta, 1548.

GREGORIUS IX. *Decretales Gregorii IX una cum glossis.* Editio ad exemplar romanum. Venetiis, 1604.

HINCMARUS REMENSIS. *Epistola ad Archiepiscopos Rodolfum et Frotarium, de nuptiis Stephani,* in *Patrologia latina.* Ed. J.-P. Migne. Vol. 126. Parisiis, 1853.

IVO CARNUTENSIS. *Decretum,* in *Patrologia latina,* Ed. J.-P. Migne. Vol. 161. Parisiis, 1855.

————. *Panormia,* in *Patrologia latina.* Ed. J.-P.Migne. Vol. 161. Parisiis, 1855.

*Liber poenitentialis Theodori Cantuariensis,* in *Die Canones Theodori Cantuariensis und ihre Überlieferungsformen.* Ed. Paul Willem Finsterwalder. Weimar: Hermann Böhlaus Nachfolger, 1929.

PAUCAPALEA. *Summa.* Ed. Johann Friedrich von Schulte. Giessen, 1890. [Photo-offset: Aalen, Scientia Verlag, 1965.]

PETRUS LOMBARDUS. *Libri IV Sententiarum.* Ed. studio et cura PP. Collegii S. Bonaventurae ad Claras Aquas. Florentiae: Quaracchi, ²1916.

POTTHAST, AUGUSTUS. *Regesta Pontificium Romanorum inde ab anno post Christum natum 1198 ad annum 1304.* Berolini, 1874-75 [photo offset: Graz, 1957].

---

* This bibliography lists only those works actually consulted. Included among the primary sources are those historical works composed before 1210.

*Quinque compilationes antiquae.* Ed. Aemilius Friedberg. Lipsiae: bei Bernhard Tauchnitz, 1882. [Photo-offset: Graz: Akademische Druck-und-Verlagsanhalt, 1956.]

ROLANDUS. *Sententiae, in Die Sentenzen Rolands nachmals Papstes Alexander III.* Ed. A. Gietl. Freiburg im Briesgau, 1891.

RUFINUS. *Summa Decretorum, in Die Summa Decretorum des Magister Rufinus.* Ed. Heinrich Singer. Paderborn: Druck und Verlag von Ferdinand Schöningh, 1902.

*Sacrae Romanae Rotae Decisiones seu Sententiae quae prodierunt annis 1909-1964.* 56 vol. Romae (post 1929 in Civitate Vaticana): Typis Polyglottis Vaticanis, 1912-1973.

STEPHANUS TORNACENSIS. *Die Summa des Stephanus Tornacensis über das Decretum Gratiani.* Ed. Joh. Friedrich von Schulte. Giessen, 1891.

*The Summa Parisiensis on the Decretum Gratiani.* Ed. Terence McLaughlin. Toronto: Pont. Institute of Medieval Studies, 1952.


B. *Reference Works*

AERTNYS, JOSEPH - DAMEN, C. *Theologia moralis.* Ed. J. Visser. Roma: Marietti, [17]1956.

ALBERTUS MAGNUS. *Opera Omnia.* E. A. Borgnet Vol. XXX: *Commentarium in IV Sent. D. 23-50* Parisiis, 1894.

ALESANDRO, JOHN. *Gratian's Notion of Marital Consummation.* Excerpts from a dissertation for the Pontificia Universitas Gregoriana. Rome: Officium Libri Catholici, 1971.

ALPHONSUS DE LIGUORI. *Theologia moralis.* Ed. Leonardus Gaudé. Vol. I, IV. Romae: Typographia Vaticana, [2]1912.

ANTONIUS A BUTRIO. *In libros decretalium commentarii.* Tom. VI. Venetiis: apud Iuntas, 1578.

BALLERINI, ANTONIUS - PALMIERI, DOMINICUS. *Opus theologicum morale.* Vol. II. Prati: ex officina Libraria Giachetti, filii et soc., [3]1899.

BANES, DOMINICUS. *Decisiones de iure de iustitia.* Tom. IV. Duaci: ex typographia Petri Borremans, [4]1615.

BANK, JOSEPH. *Connubia canonica.* Romae-Friburgi Brisgoviae - Barcinone: Herder, 1959.

BARBOSA, AUGUSTINUS. *Collectanea doctorum in ius pontificium universum.* Vol. II. Lugduni: sumptibus Anisson et Posuel, [2]1716.

BONACINA, MARTINUS. *Opera omnia.* Tom. I: *Tractatus de magno matrimonii sacramento.* Tom. II: *De legibus, deque Decalogi et Ecclesiae praeceptis.* Venetiis: apud Jacobum Thomasinum, 1728.

BONAVENTURA. *Opera theologica selecta.* Ed. cura PP. Collegii S. Bonaventurae ad Claras Aquas. Vol. IV: *Liber IV Sententiarum.* Florentiae: Quaracchi, [2]1949.

BRENKLE, JOHN J. *The Impediment of Male Impotence with Special Application to Paraplegia.* Dissertation submitted to Catholic University of America. Washington, D.C.: Catholic University of America Press, 1963.

CAPPELLO, FELIX. *Tractatus canonico-moralis de sacramentis.* Vol. V: *De matrimonio.* Romae: Marietti, [7]1961.

CASTRO PALAO, FERDINAND. *Opus morale, de virtutibus et vitiis contrariis.* Pars 5ª. Lugduni: sumptibus Joannis Antonii Hugetan et Guillelmi Barbier, ²1649.

CHELODI, IOANNIS. *Ius matrimoniale iuxta codicem iuris canonici.* Tridenti, ³1921.

CONTE A CORONATA, M. *Tractatus canonicus de sacramentis.* Vol. III: *De matrimonio et de sacramentalibus.* Romae: Marietti, ³1957.

COVARRUVIAS A LEYVA, DIDACUS. *Opera omnia.* Ed. Ioannis Uffelli. Tom. II. Lugduni: sumptibus Horatii Boissot et Georgii Remeus, 1661.

DAUVILLIER, JEAN. *Le mariage dans le droit classique de l'Église depuis le décret de Gratian (1140) jusqu'à la mort de Clément V (1314).* Paris: Librairie du Recueil Sirey, 1933.

d'AVACK, PIETRO A. *Cause di nullità e di divorzio nel diritto matrimoniale canonico.* Vol. I. Firenze: Casa Editrice del Dott. Carlo Cya, ²1952.

DE CONINCK, AEGIDIUS. *De sacramentis et censuris.* Tom. II. Lugduni: sumptibus Claudii Landry, 1619.

DE LUGO, IOANNIS. *De iustitia et iure.* Tom. I. Lugduni: sumptibus Petri Prost, 1642.

DE SMET, A. *Tractatus theologico-canonicus de sponsalibus et matrimonio.* Brugis, 1927.

DOLCIAMORE, JOHN (ed.). *Matrimonial Jurisprudence, United States 1968-71.* Hartford: Canon Law Society of America, 1973.

DURANDUS A SANCTO PORCIANO. *Petri Lombardi Sententias theologicas commentariorum libri IV.* Venetiis: ex typografia Guerraea, 1571. [Photo offset: Ridgewood, N.J.: The Gregg Press, Inc., 1964. Vol. 2.]

ENGEL, LUDOVICUS. *Collegium universum iuris canonici.* Venetiis, ⁹1760.

ESMEIN, A. - GENESTAL, R. *Le mariage en droit canonique.* Vol. I. Paris: Librairie du Receuil Sirey, ²1929.

FEDELE, PIO. *Problemi di diritto canonico, l'impotenza.* Rome: Catholic Book Agency, 1962.

FERRARIS, LUCIUS. *Prompta bibliotheca canonica, iuridica, moralia, theologica, etc.* Romae, ²1788.

FORD, JOHN. *The Validity of Virginal Marriage.* Dissertation submitted to the Pontifical Gregorian University. Worcester, Mass.: Harrigan Press, 1938.

FRATTIN, PIETRO. *The Matrimonial Impediment of Impotence: Occlusion of Spermatic Ducts and Vaginismus.* Dissertation submitted to the Catholic University of America. Washington, D.C.: Catholic University Press, 1958.

FREISEN, JOSEPH. *Geschichte des canonischen Eherechts bis zum Verfall der Glossenlitteratur.* Paderborn: Druck und Verlag von Ferdinand Schöningh, 1893.

GASPARRI, PIETRO. *Tractatus canonicus de matrimonio.* Vol. I. Romae, ²1932.

GENICOT, EDUARDUS. *Theologiae moralis Institutiones.* I-II. Lovanii: typis et sumptibus Pollneunis et Centerick, ³1900.

GONZÁLEZ-TÉLLEZ, E. *Commentaria perpetua in singulos textus quinque librorum decretalium Gregorii IX.* Venetiis: apud Nicolaum Pezzana, ²1766.

GUTIÉRREZ, IOANNIS. *Canonicae quaestiones tam ad sponsalia de futuro quam matrimonia eorumque impedimenta pertinentes.* Venetiis: apud Iuntas, 1618.

HEALY, EDWIN. *Moral Guidance.* Chicago, 1942.

──. *Medical Ethics.* Chicago: Loyola University Press, 1956.

HENRÍQUEZ, HENRICUS. *Summae theologiae moralis.* Venetiis: apud haeredes Melchioris Sessae, 1600.

HERVADA, FRANCISCO JAVIER. *La impotencia del varón en el derecho matrimonial canónico.* Pamplona, 1959.

HIQUAEUS, ANTONIUS (commentator). In IOANNIS DUNS SCOTUS. *Opera omnia.* Vol. IX: *Quaestiones in lib. IV Sententiarum.* Ed. cura Fr. Minorum Hibernorum Regularis Observantiae Collegii S. Isidori Romae. Lugduni: sumptibus Laurentii Durand, 1639.

HOLBÖCK, CAROLUS. *Tractatus de iurisprudentia Sanctae Romanae Rotae.* Graetiae-Vindobonae-Coloniae: in Officina Styria, 1957.

HOSTIENSIS [Henricus de Segusio]. *Summa aurea.* Cum adnot. F. Martini Abbatis. Lugduni, 1568.

──. *Summa aurea.* Ed. et adnot. Nicolaii Superantius. Venetiis: apud Iuntas, 1581.

INNOCENT IV [Sinibaldus Fliscus]. *Commentaria in V libros decretalium.* Ed. Leonardus a Lege. Venetiis, 1570.

IOANNIS ANDREAE. *In IV decretalium librum novella commentaria.* Ed. Petrus Vendramaenus. Venetiis: apud Franciscus Franciscum, Senensem, 1581.

IOANNIS DUNS SCOTUS. *Opera omnia.* Vol. IX: *Quaestiones in lib. IV Sententiarum.* Ed. cura Fr. Minorum Hibernorum Regularis Observantiae Collegii S. Isidori Romae cum commentario Antonii Hiquaei Lugduni: sumptibus Laurentii Durand, 1639.

JEMOLO, A. C. *Il matrimonio nel diritto canonico.* Milano: Casa Editrice Dr. Francesco Vallardi, 1941.

JOYCE, GEORGE. *Christian Marriage: An Historical and Doctrinal Study.* London: Sheed and Ward, [2]1948.

KEATING, JOHN R. *The Bearing of Mental Impairment on the Validity of Marriage.* Rome: Gregorian University Press, 1963. [1973 Reprint]

KELLY, G. *Medico-Moral Problems.* St. Louis, Mo.: Catholic Hospital Association, 1959.

KENNY, JOHN P. *Principles of Medical Ethics.* Westminster, Md.: Newman Press, 1961.

LAYMANN, PAULUS. *Ius canonicum seu commentaria in libros decretalium.* Dilingae, 1666.

──. *Theologia moralis.* Venetiis: apud Blasium Maldura, 1719.

LESSIUS, LEONARDUS. *De iustitia et iure.* Lugduni: sumptibus Claudii Larjot, typography Regii, 1622.

MCALLISTER, JOSEPH. *Ethics.* Philadelphia, [2]1955.

MCCARTHY, JOHN. *The Matrimonial Impediment of Impotence with Special Reference to the Physical Capacity for Marriage of an "Excised Woman" and "Doubly Vasectomized Man."* Rome, Officium Libri Catholici, 1948.

MCFADDEN, CHARLES. *Medical Ethics.* Philadelphia, [4]1956.

MERKELBACH, B. *Summa theologiae moralis.* Vol. III: *De sacramentis.* Brugis: Desclée de Brouwer, [10]1956.

MICHIELS, GOMMARUS. *Normae generales iuris canonici.* Vol. I. Parisiis-Tornaci-Romae: Desclée et soc., ²1949.

NAVARRUS [Martinus ab Azpilcueta]. *Consiliorum sive responsorum.* Romae: ex typographia Jacobi Tornerii, 1590.

NOLDIN, H. - SCHMITT, A. *Summa theologiae moralis.* Vol. II: *De praeceptis Dei et Ecclesiae.* Oeniponte-Lipsiae: sumptibus et typis Feliciani Rauch, ²⁷1941.

O'DONNELL, THOMAS J. *Morals in Medicine.* Westminster, Md.: Newman Press, ²1959.

PANORMITANUS ABBAS [Nicolaus de Tudeschis]. *Commentaria in libros decretalium.* Ed. Jacobus Anelli de Bottis. Tom. VII. Venetiis: apud Iuntas, 1588.

PAQUIN, JULES. *Morale et médecine.* Montreal, 1955.

PAYEN, P. G. *Déontologie médicale d'après le droit natural.* Zi-Ka-Wei (Chang-hai), 1935.

PÉREZ AB UNANOA, MARTINUS. *Opus morale theologicum de sancto matrimonii sacramento.* Lugduni: sumptibus haer.. Petri Prost, Philippi Borde, Laurentii Arnaud, 1646.

PICHLER, VITUS. *Ius canonicum secundum quinque decretalium titulos.* Pisauri, ²1758.

PIRHING, E. *Ius canonicum.* Tom. IV: *De sponsalibus et matrimonio.* Dilingae: typis et sumptibus Ioannis Caspari Bencard, 1678.

PONTIUS, BASILIUS. *De sacramento matrimonii tractatus.* Lugduni: sumptibus haered. Gabr. Boissat et Laurentii Anisson, 1640.

PRÜMMER, DOMINICUS. *Manuale theologiae moralis.* Ed. Engelbert Münch. Vol. III. Friburgi Brisgoviae-Barcinone, ¹²1955.

REGATILLO, EDUARDUS F. *Ius sacramentarium.* Santander: Sal. Terrae, ³¹1960.

REIFFENSTUEL, ANACLETUS. *Ius canonicum universum.* Tom. IV. Antverpiae: sumptibus Societatis O. M. Franc., ²1755.

RICARDUS DE MEDIAVILLA. *Super quatuor libros Sententiarum.* Ed. Ludovicus Silvestrius a Sancto Angelo in Vado. Tom. IV. Brixiae, 1591.

ROBERTI, F. - PALAZZINI, P. *Dizionario di teologia morale.* Vol. I. Roma: Studium Editrice, ⁴1968.

RONCAGLIA, COSTANTINUS. *Universa moralis theologia.* Tom. II. Lucae: ex typographia Leonardi Venturini, 1730.

ROSSET, MICHAEL. *De sacramento matrimoni, tractatus dogmaticus, moralis, canonicus liturgicus et iudiciarius.* Tom. II. Parisiis, 1895.

RAYMUNDUS DE PENNAFORT. *Summa.* Ed. secundum Honoratum Laget, Veronae: ex typographia Seminarii, apud Augustinum Carattonium, ²1744.

SALMANTICENSES. *Cursus theologiae moralis Ff. Discalceatorum B. Mariae de Monte Carmeli Collegii Salmanticensis.* Tom. II. Venetiis: apud Nicolaum Pezzana, ²1714.

SANCHEZ, THOMAS. *Disputationum de sancto matrimoni sacramento.* Antverpiae: apud Henricum Aertssium, 1626.

SCHMALZGRUEBER, FRANCISCUS. *Ius ecclesiam universum.* Vol. IX. Romae: ex typographia Rev. Cam. Apostolicae, 1845.

SCHMIER, FRANCISCUS. *Iurisprudentia canonico-civilis seu ius canonicum universum.* Tom. III. Salisburgi: impensis Ioannis Iosephi Mayr, ²1729.

SOTO, DOMINICUS. *In Quartum Sententiarum.* Vol. II. Venetiis: apud Io. Mariam Lenum, 1575.

STICKLER, ALPHONSUS. *Historia Iuris Canonici Latini.* Vol. I: *Historia Fontium.* Augustae Taurinorum: apud Custodiam Librariam Pontif. Athenaei Salesiani, 1950.

SYLVESTER PRIERAS [Sylvester Mazolini]. *Summa Sylvestrina.* Ed. P. Vendramaeno. Venetiis: apud Fabrium et Augustinum Zoppinos Fratres, ²1581.

THOMAS AQUINAS. *Opera.* Vol. XI: *Commentarius posterior super libros Sententiarum Petri Lombardi.* Ed. Ioannis Nicolaus. Parisiis: apud Societatem Bibliopolarum, 1660.

──── . *Supplementum Tertiae Partis Summae Theologicae.* Ed. Leonina. Romae: Marietti, 1956.

TOBIN, WILLIAM. *Homosexuality and Marriage.* Rome: Catholic Book Agency, 1964.

TOURNELY, HONORATUS. *De universa theologia morali.* Tom. II, III. Venetiis: apud Nicolaum Pezzana, 1746.

UBACH, JOSEPH. *Theologia Moralis.* Vol. I. Bonis Auris, ²1935.

VAN HOVE, A. *De legibus ecclesiasticis.* Vol. I. Mechlinae-Romae, 1930.
──── . *Prolegomena.* Vol. I. Mechlinae-Romae: Dessain, ²1945.

VICTORIA, FRANCISCUS DE. *Relectionum theologicarum.* II: *Relectio de homicidio.* Lugduni: apud Iacobum Boyerium, 1557. Reproduced by photo-offset in *Relecciones teológicas del Maestro Fray Francisco de Vitoria.* Ed. Luis G. Alonso-Getino. Tom. III. Madrid: Imprenta la Rafa, 1935.

WERNZ, F. X. *Ius decretalium.* Vol. IV²: *Ius matrimoniale.* Prati: ex officina libraria Giachetti, filii et soc., ²1912.

WERNZ, F. X. - VIDAL P. - AGUIRRE, P. *Ius canonicum.* Vol. V: *Ius matrimoniale.* Romae: apud aedes Universitatis Gregorianae, ³1946.

WRENN, LAWRENCE. *Annulments.* Hartford: Canon Law Society of America, ²1972.


## C. *Articles*


AGUIRRE, P. "De impotentia viri iuxta iurisprudentiam rotalem,", *Periodica,* 36 (1947), 1-23.

ALLERS, RUDOLPH. "Some Medico-Psychological Remarks on C. 1068, 1081, 1087," *The Jurist,* 4 (1944), 351-380.

BRIDE, A. "Empêchements de mariage," *Dictionnaire de droit canonique,* V, col. 261-322.

BROWN, RALPH. "A Canonical Problem of Mental Incompetence in Marriage," *The Heythrop Journal,* 10 (1969), 146-161.

CARR, AIDAN. "Moral Impotency' as a Matrimonial Impediment," *Homiletic and Pastoral Review,* 66 (1966), 1038-1040.

d'AVACK, PIETRO A. "L'impotenza generativa maschile nel diritto matrimoniale canonico," *IDE,* 62 (1951-I), 361-413.

DELHAYE, P. "The Development of the Medieval Church's Teaching on Marriage." Translated by J. Cavanagh. *Concilium,* 5 (1970), 211-231.

DE LANVERSIN, BERNARD. "Découvertes médicales récents et impuissance masculine au sens canonique du terme," *Ius Populi Dei: Miscel-*

*lanea in honorem Raymundi Bigador.* Vol. II.    Romae: apud aedes
Universitatis Gregorianae, 1972, 467-489.

DE REINA, VICTOR. "Impotencia y esterilidad," *Ius Populi Dei: Miscellanea in honorem Raymundi Bidagor.* Vol. III.    Romae: apud aedes
Universitatis Gregorianae, 1972, 441-465.

DE SMET, A. "Impuissance," *Dictionnaire de théologie catholique,* VII², 
col. 1431-1441.

DI JORIO, O. "Commentary on Pompedda 6 ottobre 1969," *IDE,* 80 (1969-
II), 147-159.

DONOVAN, JOSEPH. "Replies to Questions," *Homiletic and Pastoral Review,* 49 (1949), 904.

FINNEGAN, J. T. "The Current Jurisprudence Concerning Psychopathic
Personality," *The Jurist,* 27 (1967), 440-453.

———. "The Capacity to Marry," *The Jurist,* 29 (1969), 141-156.

FORD, JOHN. "The Refusal of Blood Transfusions by Jehovah's Witnesses," *The Linacre Quarterly,* 22 (1955), 3-10.

FORD, JOHN-KELLY, GERALD. "Notes on Moral Theology, 1953," *Theological Studies,* 15 (1954), 52-102.

FRATTIN, PIERO. "Impotence in Canon Law," *The Catholic Lawyer,* 9
(1963), 113-119.

GOODWINE, JOHN (discussion leader). "The Physician's Duty to Preserve

FORD, JOHN - KELLY, GERALD. "Notes on Moral Theology, 1953," *Theological Society,* 7 (1952), 125-138.

HARRINGTON, PAUL. "The Impediment of Impotency and the Notion of
Male Impotency," *The Jurist,* 19 (1959), 29-66, 187-211, 309-351, 465-
497.

HARRINGTON, P.-DOYLE, J. "Indications and Proof of Non-Consummation,"
*The Linacre Quarterly,* 19 (1952), 61-76.

HARRINGTON, PAUL - KICKAM, CHARLES. "The Impediment of Impotency
and the Condition of Male Impotence," *The Linacre Quarterly,* 25
(1958), 13-22; 26 (1959), 13-22, 61-73, 100-110, 143-165.

HUIZING, PETRUS. "Some Proposals for the Formation of Matrimonial
Law: Impediments, Consent, Form. I," *The Heythrop Journal,* 7
(1966), 161-182.

——— (relator). "De Matrimonio," *Communicationes,* 3 (1971), 69-81.

KEATING, JOHN R. "The Caput Nullitatis in Insanity Cases," *The Jurist,*
22 (1962), 391-411.

———. "Marriage of the Psychopathic Personality," *Chicago Studies,*
3 (1964), 19-38.

———. "Sociopathic Personality," *The Jurist,* 25 (1965), 429-438.

———. "The Legal Test of Marital Insanity", *Studia Canonica,* 1 (1967),
21-36.

KELLEHER, STEPHEN. "Relative and Absolute Incapacity to Marry," *The
Jurist,* 29 (1969), 326-331.

KELLY, GERALD. "The Duty of Using Artificial Means of Preserving Life,"
*Theological Studies,* 11 (1950), 203-220.

———. "The Duty to Preserve Life," *Theological Studies,* 12 (1951), 550-
556.

LE BRAS, G. "La doctrine du mariage chez les théologiens et les canonistes depuis l'an mille", s. v. "Mariage", in *Dictionnaire de théologie
catholique,* IX², col. 2044-2335.

LEFEBVRE, CHARLES. "Pauli VI verba de rotali iurisprudentia," *Periodica*, 58 (1969), 117-142.

——. "L'impuissance: science médicale et jurisprudence rotale," *L'an-née canonique*, 15 (1971), 415-427.

LESAGE, GERMAIN. "Psychic Impotence, a Defect of Consent," *Studia Canonica*, 4 (1970), 61-78.

McCARTHY, JOHN. "The Impediment of Impotence in the Present Day Canon Law," *Ephemerides Iuris Canonici*, 4 (1948), 96-130.

——. "Towards a Definition of Impotence," *Irish Theological Quarterly*, 18 (1951), 72-76.

——. "Traditional Concept of the Impediment of Impotence," *ITQ*, 19 (1952), 223-233.

NAVARRETE, URBANO. " 'Incapacitas assumendi onera' uti caput autonomum nullitatis matrimonii," *Periodica*, 61 (1972), 47-80.

——. "Oportetne ut supprimatur verba 'ab extrinseco et iniuste incussum' in C. 1087 circa metum irritantem matrimonium?" *Ius Populi Dei: Miscellanea in honorem Raymundi Bidagor*. III. Romae: apud aedes Pontificae Universitatis Gregorianae, 1972, 571-593.

NOLAN, KIERAN. "The Problem of Care for the Dying," in *Absolutes in Moral Theology?* Edited by Charles Curran. Washington-Cleveland: Corpus Books, 1968, 249-260.

NOWLAN, E. "Double Vasectomy and Marital Impotency," *Theological Studies*, 6 (1945), 392-427.

OESTERLÉ, GERARD. "Impuissance," *Dictionnaire de droit canonique*, V, col. 1262-1292.

——. "Von der psychischen Impotenz," *Ephemerides Iuris Canonici*, 11 (1955), 133-134.

PINTO, JOSÉ. "De matrimonii nullitate ob psychicam incapacitatem fidem conjugalem servandi," *Periodica*, 61 (1972), 439-445.

REINHARDT, MARION. "The Incidence of Mental Disorder," *Studia Canonica*, 6 (1972), 209-225.

REINHARDT, MARION - ARELLA, G. "Essential Incompatibility as Grounds for Nullity of Marriage," *The Catholic Lawyer*, 16 (1971), 171-187.

SABATTANI, AURELIO. "L'évolution de la jurisprudence dans les causes de nullité de mariage pour l'incapacité psychique," *Studia Canonica*, 1 (1967), 143-161.

SHEEHY, GERARD. "Male Psychical Impotence in Judicial Proceedings," *The Jurist*, 20 (1960), 253-294.

STAFFA, DINO. "De impotentia et inconsummatione matrimonii," *Apollinaris*, 28 (1955), 391-399.

THERIAULT, M. "Neo-vagin et impuissance," *Studia Canonica*, 1 (1968), 25-76.

VAN DUIN, ADALBERTUS. "De impedimento impotentiae psychicae in iure canonico," *Apollinaris*, 23 (1950), 114-174.

VILLEGGIANTE, SEBASTIANO. "Ninfomania e cause di nullità matrimoniale," *IDE*, 71 (1960-II), 162-184.

——. "Ninfomania e difetto di consenso," *IDE*, 71 (1960-II), 315-322.

VITALE, ANTONIO. "La 'perpetuità' dell'impotenza," *IDE*, 73 (1962), 61-68.

WRENN, LAWRENCE. "Updating the Law on Marriage," *The Jurist*, 27 (1967), 267-282.

——. "An Outline of a Jurisprudence on Sociopathy," *The Jurist*, 28 (1968), 470-485.

D. *Relevant Rotal Decisions Consulted*

| | | |
|---|---|---|
| c. Persiani | 15 November 1909 | *Dec.* 1, pp. 136-141 |
| c. Sebastianelli | 17 February 1917 | *Dec.* 9, pp. 30-37 |
| c. Rossetti | 25 March 1920 | *Dec.* 12, pp. 71-94 |
| c. Rossetti | 28 May 1921 | *Dec.* 13, pp. 114-127 |
| c. Massimi | 8 March 1924 | *Dec.* 16, pp. 86-89 |
| c. Massimi | 4 August 1927 | *Dec.* 19, pp. 363-368 |
| c. Grazioli | 16 July 1930 | *Dec.* 22, pp. 409-421 |
| c. Morano | 18 April 1931 | *Dec.* 23, pp. 131-137 |
| c. Parrillo | 24 April 1933 | *Dec.* 25, pp. 257-263 |
| c. Guglielmi | 6 August 1934 | *Dec.* 26, pp. 595-602 |
| c. Mannucci | 28 January 1935 | *Dec.* 27, pp. 41-45 |
| c. Heard | 12 November 1938 | *Dec.* 30, pp. 591-597 |
| c. Canestri | 29 July 1939 | *Dec.* 31, pp. 467-478 |
| c. Quattrocolo | 3 January 1940 | *Dec.* 32, pp. 24-37 |
| c. Jullien | 16 February 1940 | *Dec.* 32, pp. 141-154 |
| c. Quattrocolo | 14 February 1941 | *Dec.* 33, pp. 1-8 |
| c. Pecorari | 31 March 1941 | *Dec.* 33, pp. 199-202 |
| c. Heard | 9 January 1943 | *Dec.* 35, pp. 16-22 |
| c. Jullien | 16 April 1943 | *Dec.* 35, pp. 297-303 |
| c. Heard | 8 January 1944 | *Dec.* 36, pp. 21-31 |
| c. Teodori | 6 March 1944 | *Dec.* 36, pp. 142-149 |
| c. Jullien | 26 June 1944 | *Dec.* 36, pp. 444-451 |
| c. Teodori | 14 March 1945 | *Dec.* 37, pp. 281-287 |
| c. Jullien | 1 June 1945 | *Dec.* 37, pp. 324-329 |
| c. Wynen | 25 October 1945 | *Dec.* 37, pp. 574-592 |
| c. Caiazzo | 2 May 1947 | *Dec.* 39, pp. 284-296 |
| c. Wynen | 29 July 1948 | *Dec.* 40, pp. 315-325 |
| c. Filipiak | 1 December 1948 | *Dec.* 40, pp. 426-428 |
| c. Teodori | 20 Decembre 1948 | *Dec.* 40, pp. 499-503 |
| c. Canestri | 4 June 1949 | *Dec.* 41, pp. 269-274 |
| c. Brennan | 25 April 1951 | *Dec.* 43, pp. 325-332 |
| c. Staffa | 12 October 1951 | *Dec.* 43, pp. 626-629 |
| c. Sabattani | 22 June 1952 | *IDE* 64 (1953-II), pp. 367-377 |
| c. Heard | 11 July 1953 | *Dec.* 45, pp. 538-541 |
| c. Heard | 15 March 1954 | *Dec.* 46, pp. 229-233 |
| c. Filipiak | 12 November 1954 | *Dec.* 46, pp. 808-817 |
| c. Wynen | 9 March 1955 | *Dec.* 47, pp. 217-226 |
| c. Fideicicchi | 25 May 1955 | *Dec.* 47, pp. 443-448 |
| c. Pasquazzi | 7 June 1955 | *Dec.* 47, pp. 488-495 |
| c. Heard | 5 July 1956 | *Dec.* 48, pp. 633-639 |
| c. Mattioli | 25 July 1956 | *Dec.* 48, pp. 734-740 |
| c. Sabattani | 21 June 1957 | *Dec.* 49, pp. 500-513 |
| c. Pinna | 2 March 1958 | *Dec.* 50, pp. 198-209 |
| c. Staffa | 25 April 1958 | *Dec.* 50, pp. 273-276 |
| c. Sabattani | 10 April 1959 | *ME* 84 (1959), pp. 616-634 |
| c. Pinna | 4 July 1959 | *Dec.* 51, pp. 350-357 |
| c. Felici | 10 July 1959 | *Dec.* 51, pp. 376-378 |
| c. Sabattani | 16 October 1959 | *Dec.* 51, pp. 428-442 |
| c. Sabattani | 24 June 1960 | *Dec.* 52, pp. 333-342 |

| | | |
|---|---|---|
| c. Lefebvre | 9 July 1960 | *EIC* 17 (1961), pp. 170-175 |
| c. Bonet | 22 December 1960 | *Dec.* 52, pp. 604-615 |
| c. Lefebvre | 23 March 1961 | *Dec.* 53, pp. 149-155 |
| c. Pinna | 31 October 1961 | *Dec.* 53, pp. 481-488 |
| c. Anné | 27 June 1962 | *Dec.* 54, pp. 334-340 |
| c. Sabattani | 22 February 1963 | *ME* 89 (1964), pp. 147-171 |
| c. Fiore | 20 December 1963 | *Dec.* 55, pp. 991-994 |
| c. Sabattani | 20 March 1964 | *Dec.* 56, pp. 253-261 |
| c. Bejan | 13 June 1964 | *Dec.* 56, pp. 468-476 |
| c. Lefebvre | 4 July 1964 | *Dec.* 56, pp. 553-558 |
| c. Sabattani | 9 October 1964 | *Dec.* 56, pp. 682-708 |
| c. Lefebvre | 26 July 1966 | *IDE* 78 (1967-II), pp. 13-37 |
| c. Anné | 17 January 1967 | *IDE* 78 (1968-II), pp. 3-12 |
| c. Lefebvre | 2 December 1967 | *ME* 93 (1968), pp.467-477 |
| c. Fagiolo | 15 March 1968 | *IDE* 79 (1968-II), pp.264-274 |
| c. Anné | 16 July 1968 | *ME* 94 (1969), pp. 408-416 |
| c. Di Felice | 28 November 1968 | *ME* 94 (1969), pp. 96-107 |
| c. Anné | 25 February 1969 | *ME* 96 (1971), pp. 21-39 |
| c. Pompedda | 6 October 1969 | *IDE* 80 (1969-II), pp. 146-159 |
| c. Pompedda | 10 June 1970 | *ME* 96 (1971), pp. 203-219 |
| c. Di Felice | 12 December 1970 | *ME* 96 (1971), pp. 40-50 |
| c. Anné | 26 January 1971 | *IDE* 83 (1972-II), pp. 3-7 |
| c. Pinto | 18 March 1971 | *Periodica* 61 (1972), pp. 439-445 |
| c. Anné | 30 March 1971 | *IDE* 83 (1972-II), pp. 7-11 |
| c. Di Felice | 13 May 1972 | *ME* 98 (1973), p. 104 |
| c. Lefebvre | 16 December 1972 | *Periodica* 62 (1973), pp. 403-412 |
| c. Lefebvre | 15 January 1972 | *EIC* 28 (1972), pp. 319-324 |
| c. Di Felice | 13 May 1972 | *ME* 98 (1973), pp. 104-111 |

E. *Unpublished Rotal Decisions Consulted*

| | | |
|---|---|---|
| c. Palazzini | 3 February 1971 | P.N. 10,053 27/71 |
| c. Anné | 16 February 1971 | P.N. 9557 33/71 |
| c. Bejan | 24 March 1971 | P.N. 9853 5/71 |
| c. Serrano | 7 June 1971 | P.N. 10,297 126/71 |
| c. Merceica | 23 June 1971 | P.N. 10,200 154/71 |
| c. Pompedda | 5 July 1971 | P.N. 10,209 147/71 |
| c. Lefebvre | 10 July 1971 | P.N. 10,022 159/71 |
| c. Parisella | 22 July 1971 | P.N. 9795 167/71 |
| c. Masala | 13 October 1971 | P.N. 8543 177/71 |
| c. Serrano | 22 October 1971 | P.N. 10,321 187/71 |
| c. Ewers | 30 October 1971 | P.N. 10,133 198/71 |
| c. Bejan | 1 December 1971 | P.N. 8923 255/71 |
| c. Lefebvre | 4 December 1971 | P.N. 9478 227/71 |

# INDEX